DOES CHALCEDON DIVIDE OR UNITE?

DOES CHALCEDON DIVIDE OR UNITE?

Towards Convergence in Orthodox Christology

Edited by
Paulos Gregorios
William H. Lazareth
Nikos A. Nissiotis

WORLD COUNCIL OF CHURCHES, GENEVA

ISBN: 2-8254-0681-3
Cover design: Nelly Witte-Brooymans
© 1981 World Council of Churches, 150 route de Ferney,
1211 Geneva 20, Switzerland
Printed in Switzerland

Contents

Preface vii
        Rev. Prof. William H. Lazareth

Introduction: the Four Unofficial Conversations: an Experience of Joy and Hope ix
        *Metropolitan Paulos Mar Gregorios
and Prof. Nikos Nissiotis*

The Agreed Statements: Aarhus 1964, Bristol 1967, Geneva 1970, Addis Ababa 1971 1

Participants in the Consultations and Papers not Printed in this Volume 17

ESSAYS

I. The Problem of the Unification of the Non-Chalcedonian Churches of the East with the Orthodox on the Basis of Cyril's Formula: *Mia Physis tou Theou Logou Sesarkomene* (and Discussion Notes) 29
        Prof. Johannes N. Karmiris

II. St. Cyril's "One Physis or Hypostasis of God the Logos Incarnate" and Chalcedon (and Discussion Notes) 50
        The Very Rev. Prof. John S. Romanides

III. One Incarnate Nature of God the Word (and Discussion Notes) 76
        The Rev. Prof. V. C. Samuel

IV. Christology in the Liturgical Tradition of the Armenian Church (and Discussion Notes) 93
        The Very Rev. Dr. Mesrob K. Krikorian

V. The Orthodox Faith in the Liturgies and Prayers of the Coptic Church (and Discussion Notes) 107
        Dr. Hakim Amin

VI.	The Christological Dogma and its Terminology (and Discussion Notes)	121
	The Rev. Prof. Georges Florovsky	
VII.	Ecclesiological Issues Concerning the Relation of Eastern Orthodox and Oriental Orthodox Churches ...	127
	Metropolitan Paulos Mar Gregorios	
VIII.	Ecclesiological Issues Inherent in the Relations between Eastern Chalcedonian and Oriental non-Chalcedonian Churches	138
	Prof. John D. Zizioulas	

Preface

What is the Orthodox Church's conception of unity? In faithfulness to that understanding, what practical steps might now be taken to overcome the 1500-year schism between those "Eastern" Orthodox who have affirmed, and those "Oriental" Orthodox who have rejected, the Christological dogma declared by the Council of Chalcedon in 451 (One Person in Two Natures, which are united unconfusedly, unchangeably, indivisibly and inseparably)?

One good way of describing the Orthodox vision of unity was suggested to Section II (What Unity Requires) at the World Council of Churches' Nairobi Assembly (1975):

"The one Church is to be envisioned as a conciliar fellowship of local churches which are themselves truly united. In this conciliar fellowship, each local church possesses, in communion with the others, the fullness of catholicity, witnesses to the same apostolic faith, and, therefore, recognizes the others as belonging to the same Church of Christ and guided by the same Spirit.

"As the New Delhi Assembly pointed out, they are bound together because they have received the same baptism and share in the same eucharist; they recognize each other's members and ministries. They are one in their common commitment to confess the Gospel of Christ by proclamation and service to the world. To this end, each church aims at maintaining sustained and sustaining relationships with her sister churches, expressed in conciliar gatherings whenever required for the fulfilment of their common calling."

Inspired by so rich and profound a view of "conciliar fellowship", Eastern and Oriental Orthodox theologians have periodically gathered to try to "witness to the same apostolic faith", in order to heal their grievous schism. With the active support of the World Council's Faith and Order Commission, the most recent prolonged attempt took place in four unofficial consultations between 1964-1971. This volume provides the general reader for the first time with an easily accessible survey of selected essays, discussions and mutually agreed statements that climax in the historic ecumenical affirmation:

"We recognize in each other the one orthodox faith of the Church.... On the essence of the Christological dogma we found ourselves in full agreement. Through the different terminologies used by each side, we saw the same truth expressed."

Such a momentous discovery, benefitting from the wealth of recent Patristic research, is of course difficult for many to assimilate quickly. After over fifteen centuries of alienation, it is understandable that few official steps have been taken to implement the doctrinal unity documented in these pages. Moreover, the separation was frequently aggravated during the 1970s by many non-doctrinal factors that strongly affected the lives of the two different Church traditions of Eastern Christianity.

Providentially, there are new impulses of the Spirit abroad today. Throughout 1981, Christians in all parts of the world have been celebrating the 1600th anniversary of the Council of Constantinople and its unity-strengthening Niceno-Constantinopolitan Creed. In marking that significant event, Faith and Order published *Spirit of God—Spirit of Christ* to contribute to the healing of the breach (Filioque) between the Eastern and Western parts of the Church. In a similar vein we now also make available this important study in fulfilment of our mandate "to call the Churches to the goal of visible unity in one faith and one eucharistic fellowship".

WILLIAM H. LAZARETH

Introduction

The Four Unofficial Conversations:
an Experience of Joy and Hope

The distinction between "Eastern" and "Oriental" Orthodox Churches is often not only untranslatable into other languages, but also unfamiliar even to English-speaking people. It is a convention recently established for distinguishing between the two different Church traditions of Eastern Christianity.

With the term "Eastern" we refer to the one Church which is constituted by the four ancient Patriarchates (Constantinople, which enjoyed a primacy of love and honour, Alexandria, Antioch, Jerusalem), the modern Patriarchates of Russia, Rumania, Serbia and Bulgaria, and the autocephalous Churches like Cyprus, Greece, Poland, and so on. This distinction in autocephalous Churches has been made from ancient times for administrative reasons, although these Churches compose one Church communion, fully identifying doctrine and Church life throughout the whole of the Christian era, and recognizing as expressions of this identity of the One Apostolic Faith, the seven Ecumenical Councils. Due to the great movement of emigration, the "Eastern" Church is spread throughout the whole world today.

With the term "Oriental" we refer to the five ancient Churches of Egypt, Syria, Armenia, India and Ethiopia. They practise the same ancient tradition and are organized as autocephalous local Churches. Due to the same emigration movement during the last two centuries, the "Oriental" Churches are also to be found in all parts of the world.

The breach of ecclesiastical communion between the "Eastern" and the "Oriental" came about in the fifth and sixth centuries of our era as a result of controversies about the relation between the human and divine natures in Christ which began at the Council of Chalcedon (451) and continued for at least two centuries. These controversies involved also the whole of the Church both in the East and in the West.

The "Eastern" Church together with the Church of the West accepted the Christological "horos" of Chalcedon, acknowledging this Council as the Fourth Ecumenical Council in Church history, while the "Oriental" Churches rejected the teaching of this Council and never recognized it as the fourth one (accepting only the first three).

These two Church traditions of the East, although they have led a separate historical life, show today very great similarities in dogmatic faith, ecclesiology, liturgy and spirituality. This is due to their common fidelity to the ancient tradition, thought, life, and principles of Church authority and administration. This became evident after the great schism between Rome and the "Eastern" Church (1054). These similarities have been made more manifest in the contemporary ecumenical movement. They have encouraged reciprocal trends on both sides towards re-establishing a particular and closer relationship between them today. They have also stimulated the organization of a special dialogue for restoring full Church communion amongst them.

Throughout the 1500 years since Chalcedon, there have been several attempts at reconciliation, often undertaken by Byzantine emperors, but also by others. Several times the two sides came close to a reconciliation; but alas, to this day, the breach continues.

A new series of unofficial conversations began in 1964 in connection with the meeting of the Faith and Order Commission of the World Council of Churches in Aarhus, Denmark. Four such unofficial conversations were held:

Aarhus, Denmark: 11-15 August 1964
Bristol, England: 25-29 July 1967
Geneva, Switzerland: 16-21 August 1970
Addis Ababa, Ethiopia: 22-23 January 1971

These conversations covered most of the issues on which agreement was necessary before communion could be restored. We were privileged to be the organizers and to be among the participants of all four conversations.

The full reports of these conversations were edited by us and published by *The Greek Orthodox Theological Review*, the half-yearly official publication of the Holy Cross School of Theology, Hellenic College, 30 Goddard Avenue, Brookline, Massachusetts 02146, USA (Vol. X:2, Winter 1964-65; Vol. XIII:2, Fall, 1968; Vol. XVI:1 and 2, Spring and Fall, 1971). We are grateful to the *Review* for permission to reprint a selection of the papers and the texts of the four agreed statements. The selection is somewhat arbitrary. No selection can hope to do justice to the multifaceted richness of all the presentations and discussions which together occupy more than 600 pages.

Those of us who were present were grateful to God for the mostly joyful, at times painful, but always fruitful, learning experience of the four unofficial consultations. We want very much to share this experience with others who are interested and this is the purpose of this modest publication.

We began our joint efforts in 1962 to organize the Aarhus consultation. There was much scepticism in the beginning about the possible benefits of taking up an issue which had frustrated greater persons in previous centuries. But ours is an age of frequent ecumenical contacts, and our informal gatherings at various meetings of the World Council of Churches gave us new hope. We were both in Geneva at that time, Metropolitan Gregorios (then Fr Paul Verghese) in the General Secretariat of the World Council of Churches, and Professor Nikos Nissiotis at the Ecumenical Institute in Bossey. We are very much indebted to the Faith and Order Commission which consistently supported our efforts, viewed our meetings as a primary concern towards re-establishing Church unity and financed them. We are especially grateful to Dr. Lukas Vischer, former Director of the Secretariat of the Faith and Order Commission, who gave us encouragement and support and also took an active part in all four meetings. We express now our thanks also to the present Director of the Secretariat, Prof. William H. Lazareth, who has enthusiastically and efficiently commissioned and made possible the present publication.

Our initial success at Aarhus in 1964 was a joyful surprise. Outstanding scholars of both sides, belonging to two traditions not in communion with each other for a millenium and a half, could confess together that "we recognize in each other the one orthodox faith of the Church". We were criticized by non-participants, even by some very prominent theologians, for being too hasty in making such a statement. But most of the participating theologians were interested in pursuing the dialogue and clearing the issues. The Churches have all stood by us and encouraged us. In this connection we owe an enormous debt of gratitude for the enthusiastic support we received from His Holiness Patriarch Athenagoras of Constantinople of revered memory, and from several other heads of Churches.

From the beginning our unofficial work was meant to be preparatory for official action to be taken by the Churches themselves. It remains that, an offering to be accepted and used as deemed fit by the Churches. We have also in our third consultation in Geneva (1970) proposed a series of practical steps to be taken. In the light of our experience and discussions, we would respectfully urge our respective Church authorities to explore the ways and means for continuing the work which so hopefully started with these four unofficial consultations. We regard this question as an urgent and most profitable one in the service of Church unity as a whole. We are certain that if further official steps on behalf of our Churches were taken, we would, with the grace of God, witness an encouraging development in the near future towards sharing in the one unbroken Church tradition.

PAULOS MAR GREGORIOS
NIKOS NISSIOTIS

The Agreed Statements

FIRST UNOFFICIAL CONSULTATION
Aarhus, Denmark, 11-15 August 1964
An Agreed Statement

SECOND UNOFFICIAL CONSULTATION
Bristol, England, 25-29 July 1967
An Agreed Statement

THIRD UNOFFICIAL CONSULTATION
Geneva, Switzerland, 16-21 August 1970
Summary of Conclusions

FOURTH UNOFFICIAL CONSULTATION
Addis Ababa, Ethiopia, 22-23 January 1971
Summary of Conclusions

Aarhus 1964

AN AGREED STATEMENT

Ever since the second decade of our century representatives of our Orthodox Churches, some accepting seven Ecumenical Councils and others accepting three, have often met in ecumenical gatherings. The desire to know each other and to restore our unity in the one Church of Christ has been growing all these years. Our meeting together in Rhodos at the Pan-Orthodox Conference of 1961 confirmed this desire.

Out of this has come about our unofficial gathering of fifteen theologians from both sides, for three days of informal conversations, in connection with the meeting of the Faith and Order Commission in Aarhus, Denmark.

We have spoken to each other in the openness of charity and with the conviction of truth. All of us have learned from each other. Our inherited misunderstandings have begun to clear up. We recognize in each other the one orthodox faith of the Church. Fifteen centuries of alienation have not led us astray from the faith of our Fathers.

In our common study of the Council of Chalcedon, the well-known phrase used by our common Father in Christ, St. Cyril of Alexandria, *mia physis* (or *mia hypostasis*) *tou Theou logou sesarkomene* (the one *physis* or *hypostasis* of God's Word Incarnate) with its implications, was at the centre of our conversations. On the essence of the Christological dogma we found ourselves in full agreement. Through the different terminologies used by each side, we saw the same truth expressed. Since we agree in rejecting without reservation the teaching of Eutyches as well as of Nestorius, the acceptance or non-acceptance of the Council of Chalcedon does not entail the acceptance of either heresy. Both sides found themselves fundamentally following the Christological teaching of the one undivided Church as expressed by St. Cyril.

The Council of Chalcedon (451), we realize, can only be understood as reaffirming the decisions of Ephesus (431), and best understood in the light of the later Council of Constantinople (553). All councils, we have recognized, have to be seen as stages in an integral development and no council or document should be studied in isolation.

The significant role of political, sociological and cultural factors in creating tension between factions in the past should be recognized and studied together. They should not, however, continue to divide us.

We see the need to move forward together. The issue at stake is of crucial importance to all churches in the East and West alike and for the unity of the whole Church of Jesus Christ.

The Holy Spirit, Who indwells the Church of Jesus Christ, will lead us together to the fullness of truth and of love. To that end we respectfully submit to our churches the fruit of our common work of three days together. Many practical problems remain, but the same Spirit Who led us together here will, we believe, continue to lead our churches to a common solution of these.

Bristol 1967

AGREED STATEMENT

1. We give thanks to God that we have been able to come together for the second time as a study group, with the blessing of the authorities of our respective Churches. In Aarhus we discovered much common ground for seeking closer ties among our Churches. In Bristol we have found several new areas of agreement. Many questions still remain to be studied and settled. But we wish to make a few common affirmations.

I.

2. God's infinite love for mankind, by which He has both created and saved us, is our starting point for apprehending the mystery of the union of perfect Godhead and perfect manhood in our Lord Jesus Christ. It is for our salvation that God the Word became one of us. Thus He who is consubstantial with the Father became by the Incarnation consubstantial also with us. By His infinite grace God has called us to attain to His uncreated glory. God became by nature man that man may become by grace God. The manhood of Christ thus reveals and realizes the true vocation of man. God draws us into fulness of Communion with Himself in the Body of Christ, that we may be transfigured from glory to glory. It is in this soteriological perspective that we have approached the Christological question.

3. We were reminded again of our common Fathers in the universal Church — St. Ignatius and St. Ireneus, St. Anthony and St. Athanasius, St. Basil and St. Gregory of Nyssa and St. John Chrysostom, St. Ephrem Syrus and St. Cyril of Alexandria and many others of venerable memory. Based on their teaching, we see the integral relation between Christology and soteriology and also the close relation of both to the doctrine of God and to the doctrine of man, to ecclesiology and to spirituality, and to the whole liturgical life of the Church.

4. Ever since the fifth century, we have used different formulae to confess our common faith in the One Lord Jesus Christ, perfect God and perfect Man. Some of us affirm two natures, wills and energies hypostatically united in the One Lord Jesus Christ. Some of us affirm one united divine-human nature, will and energy in the same Christ. But both sides speak of a union without confusion, without change, without division, without separation. The four adverbs belong to our common tradition. Both affirm the dynamic permanence of the God-

head and the Manhood, with all their natural properties and faculties, in the one Christ. Those who speak in terms of "two" do not thereby divide or separate. Those who speak in terms of "one" do not thereby commingle or confuse. The "without division, without separation" of those who say "two," and the "without change, without confusion" of those who say "one" need to be specially underlined, in order that we may understand each other.

5. In this spirit, we have discussed also the continuity of doctrine in the Councils of the Church, and especially the monenergistic and monothelete controversies of the seventh century. All of us agree that the human will is neither absorbed nor suppressed by the divine will in the Incarnate Logos, nor are they contrary one to the other. The uncreated and created natures, with the fulness of their natural properties and faculties, were united without confusion or separation, and continue to operate in the one Christ, our Saviour. The position of those who wish to speak of one divine-human will and energy united without confusion or separation does not appear therefore to be incompatible with the decision of the Council of Constantinople (680-81), which affirms two natural wills and two natural energies in Him existing indivisibly, inconvertibly, inseparably, inconfusedly.

6. We have sought to formulate several questions which need further study before the full communion between our Churches can be restored. But we are encouraged by the common mind we have on some fundamental issues to pursue our task of common study in the hope that despite the difficulties we have encountered the Holy Spirit will lead us on into full agreement.

II.

7. Our mutual contacts in the recent past have convinced us that it is a first priority for our Churches to explore with a great sense of urgency adequate steps to restore the full communion between our Churches, which has been sadly interrupted for centuries now. Our conversations at Aarhus in 1964 and at Bristol in 1967 have shown us that, in order to achieve this end by the grace of God, our Churches need to pursue certain preliminary actions.

8. The remarkable measure of agreement so far reached among the theologians on the Christological teaching of our Churches should soon lead to the formulation of a joint declaration in which we express together in the same formula our common faith in the One Lord Jesus Christ whom we all acknowledge to be perfect God and perfect Man. This formula, which will not have the status of a confession of faith

or of a creed, should be drawn up by a group of theologians officially commissioned by the Churches, and submitted to the Churches for formal and authoritative approval, or for suggestions for modifications which will have to be considered by the Commission before a final text is approved by the Churches.

9. In addition to proposing a formula of agreement on the basic Christological faith in relation to the nature, will and energy of our one Lord Jesus Christ, the joint theological commission will also have to examine the canonical, liturgical and jurisdictional problems involved — e.g anathemas and liturgical deprecations by some Churches of theologians regarded by others as doctors and saints of the Church, the acceptance and non-acceptance of some Councils, and the jurisdictional assurances and agreements necessary before formal restoration of communion.

10. We submit this agreed statement to the authorities and peoples of our Churches with great humility and deep respect. We see our task as a study group only in terms of exploring together common possibilities which will facilitate action by the Churches. Much work still needs to be done, both by us and by the Churches, in order that the unity for which our Lord prayed may become real in the life of the Churches.

Bristol, July 29, 1967

Geneva 1970

1. SUMMARY OF CONCLUSIONS

1. The third unofficial consultation between the theologians of the Oriental Orthodox and Eastern Orthodox Churches was held from August 16-21, 1970 at the Cenacle, Geneva, in an atmosphere of openness and trust which has been built up thanks to the two previous conversations at Aarhus (1964) and Bristol (1967).

REAFFIRMATION OF CHRISTOLOGICAL AGREEMENT

2. We have reaffirmed our agreements at Aarhus and Bristol on the substance of our common Christology. On the essence of the Christological dogma our two traditions, despite fifteen centuries of separation, still find themselves in full and deep agreement with the universal tradition of the one undivided Church. It is the teaching of the blessed Cyril on the hypostatic union of the two natures in Christ that we both affirm, though we may use differing terminology to explain this teaching. We both teach that He who is consubstantial with the Father according to Godhead became consubstantial also with us according to humanity in the Incarnation, that He who was before all ages begotten from the Father, was in these last days for us and for our salvation born of the blessed Virgin Mary, and that in Him the two natures are united in the one hypostasis of the Divine Logos, without confusion, without change, without division, without separation. Jesus Christ is perfect God and perfect man, with all the properties and faculties that belong to Godhead and to humanity.
3. The human will and energy of Christ are neither absorbed nor suppressed by His divine will and energy, nor are the former opposed to the latter, but are united together in perfect concord without division or confusion; He who wills and acts is always the One hypostasis of the Logos Incarnate. One is Emmanuel, God and Man, Our Lord and Saviour, Whom we adore and worship and who yet is one of us.

4. We have become convinced that our agreement extends beyond Christological doctrine to embrace other aspects also of the authentic tradition, though we have not discussed all matters in detail. But through visits to each other, and through study of each other's liturgical traditions and theological and spiritual writings, we have rediscovered, with a sense of gratitude to God, our mutual agreement in the common Tradition of the One Church in all important matters - liturgy and spirituality, doctrine and canonical practice, in our understanding of the Holy Trinity, of the Incarnation, of the Person and Work of the Holy Spirit, on the nature of the Church as the Communion of Saints with its ministry and Sacraments, and on the life of the world to come when our Lord and Saviour shall come in all his glory.

5. We pray that the Holy Spirit may continue to draw us together to find our full unity in the one Body of Christ. Our mutual agreement is not merely verbal or conceptual; it is a deep agreement that impels us to beg our Churches to consummate our union by bringing together again the two lines of tradition which have been separated from each other for historical reasons for such a long time. We work in the hope that our Lord will grant us full unity so that we can celebrate together that unity in the Common Eucharist. That is our strong desire and final goal.

SOME DIFFERENCES

6. Despite our agreement on the substance of the Tradition, the long period of separation has brought about certain differences in the formal expression of that tradition. These difference have to do with three basic ecclesiological issues - (a) the meaning and place of certain Councils in the life of the Church, (b) the anathematization or acclamation as Saints of certain controversial teachers in the Church, and (c) the jurisdictional questions related to manifestation of the unity of the Church at local, regional and world levels.

(a) Theologians from the Eastern Orthodox Church have drawn attention to the fact that for them the Church teaches that the seven ecumenical Councils which they acknowledge have an inner coherence and continuity that make them a single indivisible complex to be viewed in its entirety of dogmatic definition. Theologians from the Oriental Orthodox Church feel, however, that the authentic Christological tradition has so far been held by them on the basis of the three ecumenical Councils, supplemented by the liturgical and patristic tradition of the Church. It is our hope that further study will lead to the solution of this problem by the decision of our Churches.

As for the Councils and their authority for the tradition, we all agree that the Councils should be seen as charismatic events in the life of the Church rather than as an authority over the Church; where some Councils are acknowledged as true Councils, whether as ecumenical or as local, by the Church's tradition, their authority is to be seen as coming from the Holy Spirit. Distinction is to be made not only between the doctrinal definitions and canonical legislations of a Council, but also between the true intention of the dogmatic definition of a Council and the particular terminology in which it is expressed, which latter has less authority than the intention.

(b) The reuniting of the two traditions which have their own separate continuity poses certain problems in relation to certain revered teachers of one family being condemned or anathematized by the other. It may not be necessary formally to lift these anathemas, nor for these teachers to be recognised as Saints by the condemning side. But the restoration of Communion obviously implies, among other things, that formal anathemas and condemnation of revered teachers of the other side should be discontinued, as in the case of Leo, Dioscurus, Severus, and others.

(c) It is recognised that jurisdiction is not to be regarded only as an administrative matter, but that it also touches the question of ecclesiology in some aspects. The traditional pattern of territorial autonomy or autocephaly has its own pragmatic, as well as theological, justification. The manifestation of local unity in the early centuries was to have one bishop, with one college of presbyters united in one eucharist. In more recent times pragmatic considerations, however, have made it necessary in some cases to have more than one bishop and one eucharist in one city, but it is important that the norm required by the nature of the Church be safe guarded at least in principle and expressed in Eucharistic Communion and in local conciliar structures.

7. The universal Tradition of the Church does not demand uniformity in all details of doctrinal formulation, forms of worship and canonical practice. But the limits of pluralistic variability need to be more clearly worked out, in the areas of the forms of worship, in terminology of expressing the faith, in spirituality, in canonical practice, in administrative or jurisdictional patterns, and in the other structural or formal expressions of tradition, including the names of teachers and Saints in the Church.

TOWARDS A STATEMENT OF RECONCILIATION

8. We reaffirm the suggestion made by the Bristol consultation that one of the next steps is for the Churches of our two families to appoint an official joint commission to examine those things which have separated us in the past, to discuss our mutual agreements and disagreements and to see if the degree of agreement is adequate to justify the drafting of an explanatory statement of reconciliation, which will not have the status of a confession of faith or a dogmatic definition, but can be the basis on which our Churches can take the steps necessary for our being united in a Common Eucharist.

We have given attention to some of the issues that need to be officially decided in such a statement of reconciliation. Its basic content would of course be the common Christological agreement; it should be made clear that this is not an innovation on either side, but an explanation of what has been held on both sides for centuries, as is attested by the liturgical and patristic documents. The common understanding of Christology is the fundamental basis for the life, orthodoxy and unity of the Church.

Such a statement of Reconciliation could make use of the theology of St. Cyril of Alexandria as well as expressions used in the Formula of Concord of 433 between St. Cyril and John of Antioch, the terminology used in the four later Councils and in the patristic and liturgical texts on both sides. Such terminology should not be used in an ambiguous way to cover up real disagreement, but should help to make manifest the agreement that really exists.

SOME PRACTICAL STEPS

9. Contacts between Churches of the two families have developed at a pace that is encouraging. Visits to each other, in some cases at the level of heads of Churches, and in others at episcopal level or at the level of theologians have helped to mark further progress in the growing degree of mutual trust, understanding and agreement. Theological students from the Oriental Orthodox Churches have been studying in institutions of the Eastern Orthodox Churches for some time now; special efforts should be made now to encourage more students from the Eastern Orthodox Churches to study in Oriental Orthodox institutions. There should be more exchange at the level of theological professors and church dignitaries.

It is our hope and prayer that more official action on the part of the two families of Churches will make the continuation of this series of unofficial conversations no longer necessary. But much work still needs to be done, some of which can be initiated at an informal level.

10. With this in mind this third unofficial meeting of theologians from the two families constitutes:

(a) a Continuation Committee of which all the participants of the three conversations at Aarhus, Bristol and Geneva would be corresponding members, and

(b) a Special Executive Committee of this Continuation Committee consisting of the following members, and who shall have the functions detailed further below:

  1. Metropolitan Emilianos of Calabria
  2. Archpriest Vitaly Borovoy
  3. Vardapet Mesrob Krikorian
  4. Professor Nikos Nissiotis
  5. Father Paul Verghese

FUNCTIONS:

(a) To edit, publish and transmit to the Churches a report of this third series of conversations, through the **Greek Orthodox Theological Review**.

(b) To produce, on the basis of a common statement of

which the substance is agreed upon in this meeting, a resume of the main points of the three unofficial conversations in a form which can be discussed, studied and acted upon by the different autocephalous Churches;

(c) To publish a handbook containing statistical, historical, theological and other information regarding the various autocephalous Churches;

(d) To explore the possibility of constituting an association of Theological Schools, in which all the seminaries, academies and theological faculties of the various autocephalous Churches of both families can be members;

(e) To publish a periodical which will continue to provide information about the autocephalous Churches and to pursue further discussion of theological, historical and ecclesiological issues;

(f) To make available to the Churches the original sources for an informed and accurate study of the historical developments in the common theology and spirituality as well as the mutual relations of our Churches;

(g) To sponsor or encourage theological consultations on local, regional or world levels, with a view to deepening our own understanding of, and approach to, contemporary problems especially in relation to our participation in the ecumenical movement;

(h) To explore the possibilities of and to carry out the preliminary steps for the establishment of one or more common research centres where theological and historical studies in relation to the universal orthodox tradition can be further developed;

(i) To explore the possibility of producing materials on a common basis for the instruction of our believers including children and youth and also theological text-books.

Addis Ababa 1971

1. Summary of Conclusions

The following conclusions and questions have arisen out of our informal discussions in Addis Ababa about the lifting of anathemas and the recognition of Saints:

1. We agree that the lifting of the anathemas pronounced by one side against those regarded as saints and teachers by the other side seems to be an indispensable step on the way to unity between our two traditions.
2. We are also agreed that the lifting of the anathemas would be with a view to restoring communion between our two traditions, and therefore that it presupposes essential unity in the faith between our two traditions. The official announcement by both sides that there is in fact such essential unity in faith, a basis for which is already provided by the reports of our earlier conversations at Aarhus, Bristol and Geneva, would thus appear to be essential for the lifting of anathemas.
3. We agree further that once the anathemas against certain persons cease to be effective, there is no need to require their recognition as saints by those who previously anathematized them. Different autocephalous churches have differing liturgical calendars and lists of Saints. There is no need to impose uniformity in this matter. The place of these persons in the future united church can be discussed and decided after the union.
4. Should there be a formal declaration or ceremony in which the anathemas are lifted? Many of us felt that it is much simpler gradually to drop these anathemas in a quiet way as some churches have already begun to do. Each church should choose the way most suited to its situation. The fact that these anathemas have been lifted can then be formally announced at the time of union.
5. Who has the authority to lift these anathemas? We are agreed that the Church has been given authority by her Lord both to bind and to loose. The Church which imposed the anathemas for pastoral or other reasons of that time, has

also the power to lift them for the same pastoral or other reasons of our time. This is part of the Stewardship or Oikonomia of the Church.

6. Does the lifting of an Anathema imposed by an ecumenical council call in question the infallibility of the Church? Are we by such actions implying that a Council was essentially mistaken and therefore fallible? What are the specific limits within which the infallibility of the Church with her divine-human nature operates? We are agreed that the lifting of the anathemas is fully within the authority of the Church and does not compromise her infallibility in essential matters of the faith. There was some question as to whether only another ecumenical council could lift the anathema imposed by an ecumenical council. There was general agreement that a Council is but one of the principal elements expressing the authority of the Church, and that the Church has always the authority to clarify the decisions of a Council, in accordance with its true intention. No decision of a Council can be separated from the total tradition of the Church. Each council brings forth or emphasizes some special aspect of the one Truth, and should therefore be seen as stages on the way to a fuller articulation of the truth. The dogmatic definitions of each council are to be understood and made more explicit in terms of subsequent conciliar decisions and definitions.

7. The lifting of anathemas should be prepared for by careful study of the teaching of these men, the accusations levelled against them, the circumstances under which they were anathematized, and the true intention of their teaching. Such study should be sympathetic and motivated by the desire to understand and therefore to overlook minor errors. An accurate and complete list of the persons on both sides to be so studied should also be prepared. The study should also make a survey of how anathemas have been lifted in the past. It would appear that in many instances in the past anathemas have been lifted without any formal action beyond the mere reception of each other by the estranged parties on the basis of their common faith. Such a study would bring out the variety of ways in which anathemas were imposed and lifted.

8. There has also to be a process of education in the churches both before and after the lifting of the anathemas, especially where anathemas and condemnations are written

into the liturgical texts and hymnody of the church. The worshipping people have to be prepared to accept the revised texts and hymns purged of the condemnations. Each church should make use of its ecclesiastical journals and other media for the pastoral preparation of the people.

9. Another important element of such education is the rewriting of Church history, text-books, theological manuals and catechetical materials. Especially in Church history, there has been a temptation on both sides to interpret the sources on a partisan basis. Common study of the sources with fresh objectivity and an eirenic attitude can produce common texts for use in both our families. Since this is a difficult and time-consuming project, we need not await its completion for the lifting of anathemas or even for the restoration of Communion.

10. The editing of liturgical texts and hymns to eliminate the condemnations is but part of the task of liturgical renewal. We need also to make use of the infinite variety and richness of our liturgical traditions, so that each church can be enriched by the heritage of others.

11. There seems to exist some need for a deeper study of the question: "Who is a Saint?" Neither the criteria for sainthood nor the processes for declaring a person as a Saint are the same in the Eastern and Western traditions. A study of the distinctions between universal, national and local saints, as well as of the processes by which they came to be acknowledged as such, could be undertaken by Church historians and theologians. The lifting of anathemas need not await the results of such a study, but may merely provide the occasion for a necessary clarification of the tradition in relation to the concept of sainthood.

12. Perhaps we should conclude this Statement with the observation that this is now the fourth of these unofficial Conversations in a period of seven years. It is our hope that the work done at an informal level can soon be taken up officially by the churches, so that the work of the Spirit in bringing us together can now find full ecclesiastical response. In that hope we submit this fourth report to the churches.

Participants in the Consultations and Papers not Printed in this Volume

Participants
Aarhus 1964

EASTERN ORTHODOX PARTICIPANTS:

His Grace Bishop *Emilianos* (Timiadis) of Meloa, World Council of Churches, GENEVA, Switzerland (Ecumenical Patriarchate of Constantinople)

The Very Rev. Professor G. *Florovsky* (Professor Emeritus, Harvard University), Princeton University, PRINCETON, New Jersey, U.S.A. (Greek Orthodox Archdiocese of North and South America, Ecumenical Patriarchate of Constantinople)

The Very Rev. Professor J. S. *Romanides*, Holy Cross Greek Orthodox Theological School, 50 Goddard Ave., BROOKLINE, Mass., 02146, U.S.A. (Greek Orthodox Archdiocese of North and South America, Ecumenical Patriarchate of Constantinople)

The Very Rev. Professor Vitaly *Borovoy*, World Council of Churches, GENEVA, Switzerland (Russian Orthodox Church)

The Rev. Professor J. *Meyendorff*, St. Vladimir's Orthodox Seminary, 575 Scarsdale Road, Crestwood, TUCKAHOE, N. Y., U.S.A. (Russian Orthodox Greek Catholic Church of North America)

Professor J. N. *Karmiris*, University of Athens, 20 Dionysou St., Kifissia, ATHENS, Greece (Church of Greece)

Professor G. *Konidaris*, University of Athens, 84 Academy St., ATHENS, Greece (Church of Greece)

ORIENTAL ORTHODOX PARTICIPANTS:

His Grace Archbishop *Tiran* Nersoyan, St. Nersess Armenian Theological School, Ouzoonian House, 1456 Ridge Avenue, EVANSTON, Ill. 60201, U.S.A. (Armenian Apostolic Church)

His Grace Bishop Karekin *Sarkissian*, Armenian Theological Seminary, ANTELIAS, Lebanon (Armenian Apostolic Church, Catholicosate of Cilicia)

His Grace Archbishop *Mar Severius* Zakka Iwas of Mosul, MOSUL, Iraq (Syrian Orthodox Church)

His Grace Metropolitan *Mar Thoma Dionysius,* Mount Tabor, PATHANAPURAM, Kerala, India (Orthodox Syrian Church of the East)

The Rev. Father Dr. N. J. *Thomas,* Assistant to His Grace Mar Thoma Dionysius, Mount Tabor Monastery (Orthodox Syrian Church of the East)

Like Siltanat *Habte Mariam* Worqineh, Dean of the Cathedral of the Holy Trinity, Member of His Imperial Majesty's private Cabinet, P.O. Box 3137, ADDIS ABABA, Ethiopia (Ethiopian Orthodox Church)

The Rev. Professor V. C. *Samuel,* Theological College, P.O. Box 665, ADDIS ABABA, Ethiopia (Orthodox Syrian Church of the East)

Dr. Karam Nazir *Khella,* Lecturer, Philosophische Fakultät Hamburg; Theological Faculty Cairo, Johns-Allee 65, 2 HAMBURG 13, Postfach 2655, Germany (Coptic Orthodox Church)

Dr. *Getachew* Haile, Assistant Professor, Faculty of Arts, Haile Selassie I University, P.O. Box 399, ADDIS ABABA, Ethiopia (Ethiopian Orthodox Church)

STAFF:

Dr. N. A. *Nissiotis,* Ecumenical Institute, World Council of Churches, Château de Bossey, CELIGNY (GE), Switzerland (Church of Greece)

The Rev. Father Paul *Verghese,* World Council of Churches, GENEVA, Switzerland (Orthodox Syrian Church of the East)

The Rev. Dr. Lukas *Vischer,* Research Secretary of the Faith and Order Department, World Council of Churches, GENEVA, Switzerland

Bristol 1967

EASTERN ORTHODOX

METROPOLITAN EMILIANOS TIMIADES
Geneva (Ecumenical Patriarchate)

THE VERY REV. PROF. GEORGES FLOROVSKY
U.S.A. (Ecumenical Patriarchate)

THE VERY REV. PROF. JOHN S. ROMANIDES
U.S.A. (Ecumenical Patriarchate)

ARCHPRIEST VITALY BOROVOY
Geneva (Russian Orthodox Church)

THE REV. PROF. J. MEYENDORFF
U.S.A. (Russian Orthodox Greek Catholic Church of North America)

ARCHIMANDRITE DAMASKINOS PAPANDREOU
Taizé, France (Church of Greece)

PROFESSOR GERASIMOS KONIDARIS
Athens (Church of Greece)

PROFESSOR NIKOS A. NISSIOTIS
Ecumenical Institute, Bossey (Church of Greece)

PROFESSOR N. CHITESCU
Bucharest (Rumanian Orthodox Church)

METROPOLITAN NIKODIM SLIVEN
Bulgaria (Bulgarian Orthodox Church)

PROFESSOR E. TSONIEVSKY
Sofia (Bulgarian Orthodox Church)

ORIENTAL ORTHODOX

VARDAPET ARSEN BERBERIAN
(Armenian Apostolic Orthodox Church, Etchmiadzin)

DR. K. N. KHELLA
Egypt (Coptic Orthodox Church)

VARDAPET DR. MESROB K. KRIKORIAN
Vienna (Armenian Apostolic Orthodox Church, Etchmiadzin)

ATO G. E. MIKRE SELASSIE
Ethiopia, Secretary of Standing Committee of Oriental Orthodox Churches (Ethiopian Orthodox Church)

METROPOLITAN THEOPHILOS PHILIPPOS
India (Syrian Orthodox Church)

BISHOP SAMUEL
Egypt (Coptic Orthodox Church)

THE REV. PROF. V. C. SAMUEL
India (Syrian Orthodox Church)

REV. FATHER PAUL VERGHESE
India (Syrian Orthodox Church)

Consultant
DR. LUKAS VISCHER   Representing the Faith and Order Secretariat of the World Council of Churches

Minute Secretary
THE REV. GARETH EVANS

Geneva 1970

EASTERN ORTHODOX

Dr. Athanase Arvanitis
(Church of Greece)
Archpriest Vitaly Borovoy
(Russian Orthodox Church)
Prof. Nicolae Chitescu
(Rumanian Orthodox Church)
Metropolitan Emilianos of Calabria
(Ecumenical Patriarchate of Constantinople)
Prof. Georges Florovsky
(Ecumenical Patriarchate)
Metropolitan Georges of Mount Lebanon
(Greek Orthodox Patriarchate of Antioch)
Bishop Pierre de Chersonese
(Russian Orthodox Church)
Prof. J. Karmiris
(Church of Greece)
Prof. G. Konidaris
(Church of Alexandria)
Prof. John Meyendorff
(Orthodox Church in America)
Metropolitan Nicodim of Sliven
(Bulgarian Orthodox Church)
Prof. N.A. Nissiotis
(Church of Greece)
Archim. Damaskinos Papandreou
(Ecumenical Patriarchate of Constantinople)
Prof. Bojan Piperov
(Bulgarian Orthodox Church)
Prof. John S. Romanides
(Church of Greece)
Prof. Liverii Voronov
(Russian Orthodox Church)
Dr. J.D. Zizioulas
(Church of Greece)
Prof. Ilia Zonewski
(Bulgarian Orthodox Church)

ORIENTAL ORTHODOX

Kahali Alemu C.
(Ethiopian Orthodox Church)
Very Rev. Nerses Bozabalian
(Armenian Apostolic Church)
Abba G.E. Degou
(Ethiopian Orthodox Church)
Bishop Anba Gregorius
(Coptic Orthodox Church of Egypt)
Metropolitan Severius Zakka Iwas
(Syrian Orthodox Church)
Rev. Dr. K.C. Joseph
(Syrian Orthodox Church in India)
Dr. Mesrob K. Krikorian
(Armenian Apostolic Church)
Metropolitan Mar Theophilus Philipos
(Syrian Orthodox Church in India)
Fr. T. Paul Verghese
(Syrian Orthodox Church in India)
Liqe Seltanat Habte Mariam Worqneh
(Ethiopian Orthodox Church)

Consultant

Dr. Lukas Vischer (representing the Faith and Order Secretariat of the World Council of Churches)

Addis Ababa 1971

EASTERN ORTHODOX

Metropolitan Parthenios of Carthage
(Patriarchate of Alexandria)
Metropolitan Nikodim of Leningrad
(Moscow Patriarchate)
Metropolitan Nikodim of Attica
(Church of Greece)
Metropolitan Methodios of Axum
(Patriarchate of Alexandria)
Archpriest Liverii Voronov
(Moscow Patriarchate)
Professor Sabas Agourides
(Church of Greece)
Professor Nikos Nissiotis
(Church of Greece)
Professor Todor Sabev
(Church of Bulgaria)
Archpriest Vitaly Borovoy
(Russian Orthodox Church)
Professor Panayotis Fouyas
(Church of Greece)
Dr. Andreas Mitsides
(Church of Cyprus)
Fr. Sergii Hackel
(Russian Orthodox Church)
Fr. Nicolas Osolin
(Russian Orthodox Church)

ORIENTAL ORTHODOX

Bishop Samuel
(Coptic Orthodox Church)
Bishop Karekin Sarkissian
(Armenian Apostolic Church)
Fr. Paul Verghese
(Syrian Orthodox Church of India)
Dr. V.C. Samuel
(Syrian Orthodox Church of India)
Like Seltanat Habte Mariam Workineh
(Ethiopian Orthodox Church)
Professor Mikre Selassie Gebre
Ammanuel (Ethiopian Orthodox Church)
Archimandrite Nerses Bozabalian
(Armenian Apostolic Church)
Archimandrite Shnork Kasparian
(Armenian Apostolic Church)
Dr. K. M. Simon
(Syrian Orthodox Patriarchate)
Ato. Abebaw Yigzaw
(Ethiopian Orthodox Church)
Ato. Adamu Amare
(Ethiopian Orthodox Church)
Ato. Aberra Bekele
(Ethiopian Orthodox Church)
Ato. Wolde Selassie
(Ethiopian Orthodox Church)
Ato. Ayele Gulte
(Ethiopian Orthodox Church)
Archpriest Memher Ketsela
(Ethiopian Orthodox Church)
Melake Berhanat Tesfa of Borana
(Ethiopian Orthodox Church)

CONSULTANT

Dr. Lukas Vischer (representing Faith and Order Secretariat)

MINUTES SECRETARY

The Rev. Philip Cousins

The following persons were also present:
Dejazmatch Amha Aberra (Ethiopian Orthodox Church)
Fr. Nessibu Taffesse (Ethiopian Orthodox Church)
Fr. Gebre Ighziabher Degou (Ethiopian Orthodox Church)

Papers not Printed in this Volume

The Greek Orthodox Theological Review
Vol. X, 2 Winter 1964-65

	Pages
Preface .... The Rev. Prof. John S. Romanides	7-8
Introduction .... The Rev. Paul Verghese and Prof. Nikos A. Nissiotis	9-11
Chalcedonians and Monophysites after Chalcedon (and discussion notes) .... The Rev. Prof. John Meyendorff	16-36
The Reciprocal Relation Between Doctrinal and Historical Factors in the Separation of the Oriental Churches from the Ancient Catholic Church (and discussion notes) .... Prof. G. Konidaris	54-60
The Doctrine of the Person of Christ in the Armenian Church: a brief survey with special reference to the union of the two natures (and discussion notes) .... Bishop Karekin Sarkissian	108-121
The Lesson of History on the Controversy Concerning the Nature of Christ (and discussion notes) .... Archbishop Tiran Nersoyan	122-132
The Question of Reconciliation and Reunion Between the Ancient Oriental and the Orthodox Churches ...... The Rev. Vitaly Borovoy	133-136
A Theological Approach to the Mia-Physis Christology in the Fifth Century .... Dr. K. N. Khella	137-145
Statement Made by His Grace Mar Thoma Dionysius...	146-149
The Doctrine of the Union of the Two Natures in Christ Archbishop Mar Severius Zakka Iwas................	151-153
The Mystery of the Incarnation .... The Very Rev. Like Siltanat Habte Mariam Worquineh	154-160

The Greek Orthodox Theological Review
Vol. XIII:2, Fall 1968

	Pages
From Aarhus to Bristol Metropolitan Emilianos of Calabria	137-142
Some Observations on the Aarhus Consultation (and discussion notes) Prof. P. N. Trembelas	143-151
The Manhood of Jesus Christ in the Tradition of the Syrian Orthodox Church (and discussion notes) Prof. V. C. Samuel	152-169
The Union of the Two Natures in Christ according to Non-Chalcedonian Churches and Orthodoxy (and discussion notes) Prof. Elias Tsonievsky	170-189
Monothelete Controversy: a Historical Survey (and discussion notes) Fr Paul Verghese	196-211
The Christological Dogma in Orthodox Worship (and discussion notes) Prof. John Karmiris	241-262
The Inner Continuity and Coherence of the Trinitarian and Christological Dogma in the Seven Ecumenical Councils (and discussion notes) Prof. G. Konidaris	263-277
Do the Four Later Councils Prevent Reconciliation by the Orthodox Churches? (and discussion notes) Dr. K. N. Khella	278-287
The Position of Some Orthodox and Roman Catholic Theologians on the Wills of the Person of Jesus Christ and the Problem of Relations with the Non-Chalcedonians (and discussion notes) Prof. Nicolas Chitescu	288-308
The Doctrine of One Nature in the Syrian Rites (and discussion notes) Archbishop Severius Zakka Iwas	309-315

The Greek Orthodox Theological Review
Vol. XVI:1 and 2, Spring and Fall, 1971

	Pages
A Brief History of Efforts to Reunite the Chalcedonian and Non-Chalcedonian Sides from 451-641 A.D. ...... Prof. V. C. Samuel	44-62
The Christological Decisions of Chalcedon: Their History down to the Sixth Ecumenical Synod, 451-680/ 681 .... Prof. G. Konidaris	63-78
The Distinction between the *Horoi* and the *Canons* of the Early Synods and their Significance for the Acceptance of the Councils of Chalcedon by the Non-Chalcedonian Churches .... Prof. John Karmiris	79-107
The Difference Between the *Horos* and the *Canon* and its Importance for the Reception of the Synod of Chalcedon .... Prof. N. Chitescu	108-132
The Canonical Traditions of the Orthodox Church and the Oriental Churches .... Bishop Pierre de Chersonese	163-172
A Historico-Theological Review of the Anathemata of the Fourth Ecumenical Council by the Armenian Church .... Metropolitan Damaskinos Papandreou	173-192
The First Three Ecumenical Councils and their Significance for the Armenian Church .... Vardapet Mesrob Krikorian	193-209
Condemnation of Teachers and Acclamation of Saints Prof. V. C. Samuel	236-244
Recognition of Saints and Problems of Anathemas..... Archpriest Vitaly Borovoy	245-259

Essays

THE PROBLEM OF THE UNIFICATION OF THE NON-CHALCEDONIAN CHURCHES OF THE EAST WITH THE ORTHODOX ON THE BASIS OF CYRIL'S FORMULA: "MIA PHYSIS TOU THEOU LOGOU SESARKOMENE"

PROF. JOHANNES N. KARMIRIS

Anyone will become perplexed who today objectively and unbiasedly investigates the ecclesiastical events of the fifth century A.D. occasioned by Monophysitism. This perplexity is due to the fact that one can find no sufficient dogmatic-ecclesiastical reason for their having detached themselves from the stem of the Orthodox Catholic Church of the East to which they still organically belong. If one also investigates their dogmatic teaching which developed in the following fifteen centuries together with their way of worship, their ecclesiastical structure and their government, one must conclude with astonishment that they agree with the Orthodox Catholic Church in almost all "necessaries," the exception being a vague difference of opinion with regard to the verbal formulation of the dogma of Chalcedon — a difference which is probably more terminological than real. And indeed these churches today appear to us to accept a special form of moderated Monophysitism (as it can incorrectly be named), a Monophysitism which restricts itself only to the acceptance of a divine-human nature, united and joined in Christ. Though they accept this moderated Monophysitism, they at the same time, with the Orthodox Catholic Church, condemn the archheretic, Eutyches, and his pure, unadulterated Monophysitism. This inconsistency can probably be traced to a misunderstanding of the Greek-Orthodox dogmatic terms "ousia," "physis," "prosopon," "hypostasis," "hypostatike enosis," "Logos," etc., which could not be precisely translated into the eastern national languages of the peoples to whom these churches belonged. This is the only major difference between the Orthodox and the above-mentioned venerable eastern churches, a difference which has been blunted significantly with the passing of the centuries so that one can say that it really is restricted to a difference of words and formulations. This difference increased because of the unclarity of their dogmatic doctrine and the interruption of their further dogmatic and theological development.

Similarly, the separation involves several other secondary and unessential differences, e.g. with regard to the number of ecumenical councils, the number of church fathers who are to be venerated and other liturgical and canonical differences and customs.

An opinion similar to that expressed above has remained alive among many Orthodox and many adherents of the other eastern churches from the fifth until the twentieth centuries. This can be seen

1) From the participation by certain Armenian bishops in the Fifth, Sixth and Seventh Ecumenical Councils, from the canons of the Trullanum,[1] which are concerned with the Armenians;

2) From the condemnation of the "three chapters," pronounced by the Fifth Ecumenical Council, which was received by the non-Chalcedonian churches; from the encyclical addressed to "all bishop's sees in the East" (866)[2] by the Patriarch of Constantinople, Photius;

3) From the negotiations between Byzantine and Armenian representatives in the twelfth century which were in favour of union, and particularly from the famous "discussion" of the Byzantine Theorianos with the Armenian Catholicos, Nerses IV;[3]

4) From the declaration published by the local Orthodox Synod of Jerusalem (1672)[4] in favour of the non-Chalcedonian churches;

5) And from the declaration of the Ecumenical Patriarch in 1951;[5]

6) From the amicable attitude during the meeting between Orthodox and non-Chalcedonian representatives at the First Pan-Orthodox Meeting at Rhodes in 1961.

The classical dogmatician of the Orthodox Church, John of Damascus, successfully expressed Orthodoxy's positive attitude towards the non-Chalcedonian Christians of the East when he said that he considered them, "on the basis of the Constitution of Chalcedon, to be separated from the [Orthodox] Church only with

---

[1] Joh. Karmiris, *The Dogmatic and Symbolic Monuments of the Orthodox Catholic Church* (Athens, 1960), vol. I (2), pp. 231, 233, 234.

[2] *Ibid.*, p. 322.

[3] Migne, *P.G.*, 133, 119-297. See also, B. Stefanides, *Church History* (Athens, 1948), p. 380.

[4] Joh. Karmiris, *op. cit.*, vol II (1), 1953, p. 731.

[5] *Ibid.*, vol I (2), p. 172. "Orthodoxia" (Constantinople) 26 (1951), 483, 490.

regard to their geographical position, while being Orthodox in all other things."⁶ Because of this situation, it is necessary that on both sides intensive efforts be made towards the reunion of the non-Chalcedonian churches with the Orthodox Church.

Self-evidently, all discussions and endeavours towards union must concentrate on the one serious dogmatic difference of opinion existing between them in order to eliminate it. This difference of opinion concerns the dogma of the hypostatic union of the two natures in Christ, as formulated at the Fourth Ecumenical Council. As soon as this difference is settled, the other smaller ones existing between them can easily be eliminated. With regard to this cardinal difference we believe that, provided that the dogma of Chalcedon remains untouched, a new *formula concordiae* could be found for the Orthodox Church and for the non-Chalcedonian churches separated from it which would satisfy both sides; because in regard to the essence of the dogma there does not seem to be any real difference. The entire difference of opinion of the non-Chalcedonian eastern churches is based in their traditional, monophysitizing formulation of the dogma of the union of the two natures in Christ, although these churches understand this dogma in an almost Orthodox manner, believing that the two natures, the divine and the human, "neither mixed nor changed," are united in Christ. The difference of opinion which arose at the time of the Fourth Ecumenical Council and which was confirmed thereafter, seems afterwards to have increasingly lost its incisiveness and has almost completely disappeared today. Admittedly, the separated eastern churches hesitate to acknowledge the Fourth Ecumenical Council and clearly to confess the two natures in Christ. On the other hand, they accept the two natures in all essentials, as "neither mixed nor changed nor divided," rejecting only the Chalcedonian "en duo physesi" (in two natures) after the union and holding to the "ek duo physeon" (from two natures) before the union. Therefore, we believe that the phrase of St. Cyril of Alexandria which is more used by and satisfactory to the monophysitizing churches, could be proposed as the basis for the desirable union. This phrase reads: "Mia physis tou Theou Logou sesarkomene" or the more Orthodox "sesarkomenou" (one incarnate nature of the God-Logos). In using it, it would be understood and interpreted in an Orthodox way, being generally

---

⁶ *De haeres*, 83. Migne, *P.G.*, 94, 741.

understood in terms of Cyril's doctrine of the union of the two natures in Christ.

However, how do St. Cyril and the later Orthodox fathers understand the phrase "mia physis tou Theou Logou sesarkomene"? Clearly they interpret the term "one nature" as *one* hypostasis, as *one* person of the God-Logos, who became incarnate. In other words, they view this phrase as being equivalent in meaning to the statement of John the Evangelist "the Word became flesh" (John 1:14). And, in fact, when they concerned themselves with Nestorius' false teaching of "two natures = two persons," they believed that they could answer him by emphasizing the "one nature," that is, by emphasizing the one hypostasis, the one person of the God-Logos, which was used as the basis for the hypostatic union of the divine and the human natures. As is well known, the terms "nature," "hypostasis" and "person" were equated at that time since they were regarded as synonymous and identical. For that reason, the term "nature," in the phrase in question, is to be understood as "person" in and of itself, i.e. the person of the eternal God-Logos. St. Cyril writes: ". . . the nature of the Logos, i.e. the hypostasis, which is the Logos itself."[7] By means of the preceding word "one" every Nestorian sense of a division of the one person of the incarnate Logos of God is excluded and his unity is stressed. Moreover, the participle translated by the English word "incarnate" declares that the human nature, when the fullness of time was come, was received by and hypostatically united to the eternal Logos of God. Thus, this participle occurs also in Cyril's writings both in the nominative, to agree with the word "nature," as in the phrase quoted above, and in the genitive, to agree with the phrase "of the Son and Logos," as in the following: "mia physis Huiou sesarkomenou" (one nature of the incarnate Son), and "mian einai pisteuomen ten tou Huiou physin, hos henos plen enanthropesantos kai sesarkomenou"[8] (we believe in the one nature of the Son, but as having become man and flesh). According to this, the expression "one nature" means one hypostasis, one person, but not, as Nestorius believed, two natures, i.e. two hypostases, or two persons, after the union. This is true because the "one nature," i.e. the one hypostasis of the God-Logos, "became incarnate." It is thus united without mixture with the

---

[7] Cyril of Alexandria, *Apology*, Migne, *P.G.*, 76, 401.
[8] Cyril of Alexandria, *Epist.*, 40, Migne, *P.G.*, 77, 192/3.

Unification on the Basis of Cyril's Formula 33

human nature, received fully and completely from the Virgin Mary — a human nature which never existed before and outside of the hypostatic union ("ou gar prohypostase kath' heauten sarki henothe ho Theos Logos" — because the God-Logos did not unite with a human nature, pre-existing of itself),[9] being without hypostasis (anhypostatos) and without person (aprosopos) "in contemplation" (en ennoiais); because as person it used the person, or hypostasis, of the God-Logos.[10] For this reason, the term "nature," both in Cyril's expression "one nature" and in Nestorius' term "two natures," has the meaning of hypostasis (or person) of the one who exists in and of himself, as said already. According to St. John of Damascus, St. Cyril understands by the "expression 'incarnate' the essence of the flesh; with the term 'one nature' he understands the one hypostasis of the Logos . . . i.e. his divinity. . . . Thus, they are two natures" (tou eipein sesarkomenene, ten tes sarkos ousian . . . dia de tou mian physin, ten mian hypostasin tou Logou . . . t.e. tes theotetos autou . . . hoste duo eisi physeis).[11] Cyril emphatically places the "one nature" = the one person of the incarnate God-Logos, in opposition to Nestorius' "two natures" = two persons. But he understands the one person to be the bearer of both natures, these being "neither mixed nor changed," but joined in such a way that no confusion, mixture or change, no assimilation or transition of the one into the other nature occurs: "ouch hos tes ton physeon diaphoras aneremenes dia ten henosin."[12] In this way Cyril avoided not only Monophysitism but also Apollinarianism in combatting Nestorianism.

That St. Cyril of Alexandria really uses the term "nature" in the sense of "hypostasis" or "person," i.e. with the meaning of the God-Logos himself together with the flesh united to him, is indicated often in his writings. Thus, in order to combat the Nestorians who imagine or confess "that the hypostases are separate after the indivisible union" and thus hold that there are "two Sons," he taught that the Lord, "being God by nature, became incarnate and therefore became a man, animated by a rational soul . . . on this account, all of the terms which are to be heard

---

[9] John of Damascus, *Expositio orth. fidei*, III, 2. Migne, *P.G.*, 94, 985.
[10] *Ibid.*, III, 11, *P.G.* 94, 1024/5.
[11] John of Damascus, *op. cit.*, III, 7, 8. *De comp. nat.* 3. Migne, *P.G.*, 94, 1012/3. 95, 116/7.
[12] Cyril of Alexandria, *Epist.* 4, *ad Nestor.* Migne, *P.G.*, 77, 45.

in the Gospels are to be attributed to one person, to one incarnate hypostasis of the Logos" or "to one hypostasis of the incarnate Logos because the one Jesus Christ is Lord according to the Scriptures."[13] Being used interchangeably, the terms "nature," "hypostasis" and "person" become synonymous. "One nature, therefore, one hypostasis of the incarnate God-Logos, i.e. one person, one Lord." Consequently, as Emperor Justinian confirmed, "the term 'nature' was used in place of hypostasis."[14] Thus, with regard to its contents, the phrase "one incarnate nature of the God-Logos" is Orthodox; it is only its external expression and formulation which seem to remind one slightly of Monophysitism. Thus, as already stated, the term "nature of the God-Logos" testifies to the divine nature and the term "incarnate" testifies to the human nature which is not of itself an hypostasis, but has become "enhypostatos," so to speak, in the hypostasis of the Logos. Furthermore the term "one nature" testifies to the one hypostasis (or one person) of the God-Logos, i.e. to the one God-Logos, who has become flesh according to St. John's formulation (John 1:14). The unity of the person, i.e. of the bearer of both natures, is preserved in that the entire phrase is equated with the following ones: "one God-Logos incarnate" or "only one is Christ, the Logos from the Father, with his own flesh."[15] Thus, St. Cyril assumes two complete natures from whose hypostatic union the one Christ resulted. He therefore does not hold that there is one nature in the monophysitic sense, i.e. that there is one substance of divinity and humanity — a view which was condemned by the Fifth Ecumenical Council.[16] As a result, we have here, with respect to contents, the dogma of Chalcedon about the hypostatic union of the two natures in Christ. However, it is expressed in the style of the theological school of Alexandria which emphasizes the one person of Christ, thus stressing the one Christ in antithesis to the Antiochian school which emphasized the persons — and thus two Christs — in the union and after it. Thus, Cyril of Alexandria himself, the Fifth Ecumenical Council, the Confession of the Emperor Justinian,

---

[13] Cyril of *Alexandria, Apologeticus,* Migne, *P.G.,* 76, 340; *In Joh. fragm. P.G.,* 74, 24.

[14] Emperor Justinian, *Confessio fidei,* in *Maus, Sacrorum Conciliorum . . . Collectio,* 9, 545.

[15] Cyril of Alexandria, *Epist.* 17, Migne, *P.G.,* 77, 112. Joh. Karmiris, *op. cit.,* I (2), p. 142.

[16] Joh. Karmiris, *op. cit.,* I (2), p. 195.

Leontius of Byzantium, John of Damascus and other Orthodox fathers understood the phrase "one incarnate nature of the God-Logos" in this Orthodox sense.

However, how does Cyril understand the union of the two natures (as indicated in the above-mentioned phrase) in a narrower and in a more general sense? This he explains elsewhere: "We said that the two natures united. However, we believe that after they united the nature of the Son is one, as though the division were already eliminated. And yet, this nature of the Son is that of one who has become incarnate and human. If one should say, however, that the Logos, being God, became incarnate and human, then any expectation of a change should be rejected (because he remained precisely what he was), and among us the entire, complete and unmixed union should be confessed also."[17] In this way, any type of monophysitic misunderstanding of the union is excluded. And again he wrote elsewhere that "(the Logos) being by nature God, was begotten as man, not simply in terms of connection (synapheia), as he (Nestorius) says, whereby he has an external unity in mind (and therefore a relative one), but as a union which is true although one cannot verbally grasp it and which surpasses understanding. Thus he is to be understood as the one and only one; because the nature is to be understood as a single whole after the union, i.e. as the incarnate nature of the Logos himself. That is something which we can similarly conceive of with regard to ourselves; for a human being is truly one, although he is composed of dissimilar things, i.e. of soul and body."[18] Thus, by the term "mia physis" here too he wishes to emphasize the unity of the person of the God-Logos by the phrase "one incarnate nature of the God-Logos." The unity of the person of Christ is after all the result of the hypostatic union of the two natures (without their having been mixed, merged or changed) just as the one true human being results from the union of soul and body — completely "disparate things." As our famous father and bishop, Athanasius, whose belief is a constant rule for Orthodoxy, also said in his writings: "two things, by nature unlike, have come together: i.e. divinity and humanity; the one resulting from both of these is Christ."[19]

---

[17] Cyril of Alexandria, *Epist.* 40, Migne, *P.G.*, 77, 192/3.
[18] Cyril of Alexandria, *Adversus blasphem. Nestorii*, Migne, *P.G.*, 76, 60/1. E. Schwartz, *Acta Concil.* I.1, 6, p. 33.
[19] Cyril of Alexandria, *Homil.* 8, 6. Migne, *P.G.*, 77, 572.

Furthermore, Cyril taught, that in uniting the two natures in Christ, the Orthodox "confess one Christ, one Son, the same one Lord and, accordingly, one incarnate nature of God." However, "no mixture, or synkrasis respectively, of the two natures occurred." ". . . the one nature is distinct from the other, out of both of which the one and only Christ is to be understood. Neither did they fail to recognize that where union is spoken about, it does not mean the coming together of one thing, but of two or more things which are by nature different. When we say 'union,' we thus confess the union of the flesh, which has a soul, and the Logos. And those who say 'the two natures' mean the same thing. Indeed, after the union, that which has been united cannot be divided. On the contrary, the Son is one, his nature one, as that of the incarnate Logos . . ." or, "according to the voice of John, the Logos became flesh."[20] Apparently, the phrase "his one nature" (mia physis autou) is to be thought of in connection with the preceding term "one Son" (eis Huios), as the one hypostasis of the Son, so that the unity of the person of the incarnate God-Logos was not annulled by assuming flesh — as also after the union "that which has been united can no longer be separated." Elsewhere, in countering a slanderous accusation against himself according to which he allegedly accepted, with the above-cited statements, a "mixing, i.e. alteration, or merging of the Logos with the body, i.e. a transformation of the body into the nature of divinity," he wrote that "the two natures, unmixed, unchanged and not transformed, have joined one another in indivisible union; because the flesh is flesh and not divinity even though it has become God's flesh. In the same way, the Logos is God and not flesh, even though he, according to his plan of salvation, made the flesh his own. . . . After the union we do not separate the natures from one another; nor do we divide the one indivisible Son into two Sons. But we confess that there is one Son and he is the one incarnate nature of the God-Logos, as the fathers said."[21] With the last sentence and with this teaching, Cyril combatted the Nestorian division of the one into two Sons, and expressed the Orthodox faith in the one incarnate Son, i.e. in the Son who became flesh. He confessed: "The Logos from God the Father hypostatically

---

[20] Cyril of Alexandria, *Epist.* 44, *to Eulogius the Presbyter*. Migne, *P.G.*, 77, 225.

[21] Cyril of Alexandria, *op. cit.*, 45, *to Sucensus the Bishop I*. Migne, *P.G.*, 77, 232.

united himself with the flesh and thus there is one Christ with his own flesh, i.e. he is God and man at the same time" (sarki kath' hypostasin henosthai ton ek Theou Patros Logon, hena te einai Christon meta tes idias sarkos, ton auton delonoti Theon te homou kai anthropon),[22] the bearer of both of the natures hypostatically united in him. Similarly, he condemned every idea of fusion in the union of the two natures, as also every idea of confusion, emptying (of the one into the other), reciprocal mingling, mixture, blending, mingling, change, alteration, transformation, conversion, or metastasis respectively, of those two natures.

Cyril elsewhere explained the Orthodox sense of the phrase "one incarnate nature of the God-Logos" as meaning the one God-Logos, who also assumed human nature and united himself with it. He wrote: "Again, those who distort what is correct have failed to recognize that it is in truth one incarnate nature of the Logos. Now if there is one Son who is by nature truly the Logos from God the Father who was born in a way which is inexpressible and who then, after assuming flesh (not flesh without a soul, but flesh with soul) spiritually issued from a woman as a man, then he is not to be divided into two persons or Sons, but remained one, not without flesh, nor external to a body, but having, by virtue of an indivisible union, his own (body). Anyone who says this asserts neither fusion nor a confusion nor anything else of this sort. Furthermore, such cannot be deduced from the term. If one would say to us that the only begotten Son of God became incarnate and man, that does not imply that the two natures were confused. Neither was the nature of the Logos transformed into that of the flesh, nor was that of the flesh transformed into that of the Logos. Each nature is to be thought of as remaining itself — thus according to the manner of expression offered by us. Inexpressible and impossible to grasp in words is the way in which he united himself and manifested to us the one nature of the Son, which nature, now, as I said, is the incarnate one. This is the case because the oneness is not attributed merely to that which belongs to the nature, but also to that which is joined in the synthesis which is man, consisting of body and soul. These are disparate things, differing in nature, which truly unite there and result in the one nature of the man. . . . There is, therefore, no reason to say

---

[22] Cyril of Alexandria, *op. cit.*, 17, to *Nestorius*. Migne, *P.G.*, 77, 120. Joh. Karmiris, *op. cit.*, I (2), p. 145.

that, if the one nature of the Logos had really become incarnate, then clearly a fusion and confusion would have had to take place, the human nature decreasing and disappearing. The human nature, however, was neither reduced, as they maintain, nor did it disappear. It completely suffices to assert that he became man, i.e. that he became incarnate. If we omitted this, then they would be in some way justified in their slander. Since, however, the phrase 'was incarnate' is necessarily added, where does a reduction or a sort of disappearance occur?"[23]

Herewith, Cyril declares that he does not understand the phrase "one incarnate nature of the God-Logos" in a monophysitic sense, but in an Orthodox sense. He does so in asserting that he acknowledges the human nature, complete and intact, and thus without fusion or confusion, without reduction or decrease, as well as the divine one after their union in Christ. And elsewhere he adds: "When we spoke of the one nature of the Logos, we held back and did not add the term 'incarnate' to it, but left it to the divine economy. The word 'Logos' at the same time served as a not improbable foundation to those who formulate the question of what is perfect in humanity or, how our own inherent nature exists. However, since perfection in humanity and the expression of our individual existence is brought in by the mention of the term 'incarnate,' they should cease clutching at a straw. One should condemn those who reject the divine plan and deny the incarnation by withholding from the Son perfect humanity. When one says that he became incarnate, one is confessing the fact that he became man, clearly and indubitably. As a result, this does not hinder one from thinking that 'one Son only, Christ, exists and he is God and man, perfect in divinity as in humanity . . .' "[24] According to that, therefore, they "clutch at a straw" who still today wish to understand Cyril's phrase "one incarnate nature of the God-Logos" in a monophysitic way. Because this phrase includes both natures which are hypostatically united in Christ, and it teaches quite clearly that "only one Son, Christ, exists and he is God and man, as complete in divinity as in humanity." Cyril stressed this fact repeatedly when he taught that the eternal Logos of God, incarnate in time, had received the entire and complete

---

[23] *Ibid.*, p. 241.
[24] Cyril of Alexandria, *op. cit.*, p. 244. See also, Leontius of Byzantium, *Scholien* VIII, Migne, *P.G.*, 86/1, 1253.

human nature, consisting of body and soul, from the Virgin Mary. And thus, after rejecting Monophysitism he also rejected Apollinarianism which denied to Christ's human nature its reasoning soul, or spirit (nous), and for this reason employed the contested formulation "mia physis tou Theou Logou sesarkomene." In antithesis thereto, Cyril speaks of a union of two complete and real natures, "of things, i.e. of hypostases, which are joined" (pragmaton egoun hypostaseon gegone synodos),[25] so that the Lord was composed "out of two different kinds of things" (ek duoin pragmatoin),[26] both of which retained the natural dissimilarity and disparity which they possessed before their union in him. On that account he characterized the union of the two natures only too accurately as "indescribable," "inexpressible," "inconceivable," "completely inexpressible and surpassing understanding," "extraordinary," "paradoxical," and as "a magnificent mystery which surpasses understanding" and can only be glimpsed and worshipped in faith.

It follows from all which has been said, that Cyril of Alexandria understood the one person of the incarnate God-Logos who had also assumed human nature and had united it to his divine nature, by the phrase "the one incarnate nature of the God-Logos." For that reason he states that the incarnate Logos is worthy of worship. He even employs the phrase "one incarnate nature of the God-Logos" in order thereby to teach the one way of worship in which the incarnate Logos is to be worshipped, substituting the phrase "one nature of the God-Logos which is incarnate and is worshipped" (mian physin tou Theou Logou sesarkomenen kai proskynoumenen) for the phrase "Huion proskynoumenon" (the Son who is worshipped). Thus he writes: we confess "not two natures of the one Son, one which is to be worshipped and one which is not to be worshipped, but one nature of the God-Logos which is incarnate and worshipped with his flesh in one act of worship. Neither do we confess two Sons, one of which is other than the true Son of God who is worshipped . . ."[27] Elsewhere he states that "we worship the Logos of God with his own flesh as

---

[25] Cyril of Alexandria, *To Those Who Dare to Advocate Nestorius' Doctrines,* Migne, P.G., 76, 396.
[26] Cyril of Alexandria, *Address to Theodosius* XLIV, Migne, P.G., 76, 1200.
[27] Cyril of Alexandria, *Apolog. and Prosphon.*, Migne, P.G., 76, 349. 1209. 1212.

one"[28] and that "we are accustomed to honouring the Emmanuel by means of an act of worship, not detaching, hypostatically, the body of the Logos which is united to him"[29] so that "we worship one God who is at the same time man, believing in him as in the one who consists of divinity and humanity."[30] Here it should be noted that insofar as the worship cannot be related to the nature in itself, but only to the one bearer of both natures, it follows that Cyril means the one hypostasis — and thus the one person of the incarnate God-Logos in the Orthodox and not in the monophysitic sense — by the phrase "the one incarnate nature of the God-Logos." That is, he means thereby the one God-Logos who became man and incarnate and who, together with his flesh, is worshipped in one act of worship, or as it was stated at the Fifth Ecumenical Council: "ton Theon Logon sarkothenta meta tes idias autou sarkos."[31]

From the passages quoted above, as well as from many more, one can conclude that Cyril teaches the hypostatic union of the two natures in Christ, i.e. the essential true and real union as opposed to the Nestorian " synapheia" (connection), i.e. an external, ethical and relative coexistence between the two natures. Yet, he conceives of the union as being without confusion, change or transformation and as being unchangeable, since the Logos of God "became incarnate neither by a metastasis or change, nor by a transformation into the nature of the flesh, nor by a confusion or fusion nor, as supposed by some, by a connection between two natures. Why those who suppose the latter do so is unexplained because the nature of the flesh is by nature unchangeable (atreptos) and not transformable (analloiotos)."[32] Cyril repeats in many passages of his writings that the divine and human nature remained unchanged in Christ, united "asygchytos kai atreptos." The last-mentioned adjectives were taken over by the Synod of Chalcedon. And for that reason he also agrees with the *expositio fidei* of the "Diallagai" with the Antiocheans of 433. He agreed with them in the essence of the Christological doctrine, always confess-

---

[28] Cyril of Alexandria, *Adv. Nestor.* 3, 1. Migne, P.G., 76, 121.

[29] Cyril of Alexandria, *ibid.*, p. 97.

[30] *Ibid.*, p. 60.

[31] Joh. Karmiris, *op. cit.*, I (2), p. 195.

[32] Cyril of Alexandria, *Epist.* 55, *concerning the sacred symbol*. Migne, P.G., 77, 304.

ing one Christ, perfect God and perfect man, of one substance with the Father in nature because of his divinity and of one substance with us in nature because of his humanity; because the predicates occurring in the Gospels are distinguished as divine ones and human ones, some referring to the one person of Christ, others dividing themselves between the two natures.[33] And this doctrine was accepted by the Fourth Ecumenical Council as well as by the Catholic Church in the East and in the West.

With everything which we have set forth here, we have attempted to ascertain and to interpret the deeper meaning of the famous formulation of St. Cyril of Alexandria, namely "mia physis tou Theou Logou sesarkomene." This formulation is the one to which the adherents of the non-Chalcedonian churches of the East appeal also today, in that they view it as expressing, more or less, their faith in the dogma of the union of the two natures in Christ. If our above interpretation should be regarded as correct by them, especially since it is attested to by Cyril himself and by other later authentic sources, and if the above-mentioned Christian brothers really do accept and honour the entire Christological doctrine of St. Cyril as did the Fourth Ecumenical Council of Chalcedon and the whole Church of Christ in East and West, then the agreement and finally also the reunion with the Orthodox could be based precisely upon the above-cited formulation as above interpreted, and, in general, upon the Christological doctrine of St. Cyril of Alexandria — to be sure, interpreted in the Orthodox sense. As is well known, the church, since the First Ecumenical Council, has not hesitated to employ new terms, phrases and formulations in restating former expressions and expositions of dogmatic truths. The difficult discussions about the "homoousion" which the holy fathers carried on at that great Council might serve as an eloquent example of this. Therefore, the church is not obliged to remain inflexible and to wrangle over words and phrases; it has the right to change them or to replace them with others. The only qualification is that the essence of the Orthodox dogmas, which in any case must always remain unchanged, may not be affected or altered. And so in the case in question, the Church is entitled to use a new formulation which satisfies and unites divided Christians. For that reason we believe that if the eastern Christians really accept the Christology of St. Cyril, a Christology

---

[33] Joh. Karmiris, *op. cit.*, 1 (2), pp. 154 f.

accepted by the Orthodox as well, then the agreement desired by both sides can come about on the basis of his teaching. Also, with God's help, reunification could be achieved by drawing up a Christological formula of union and a text similar to that of the "Diallagai" of 433 and corresponding to Cyril's Orthodox doctrine. This, to be sure, must be done in such a way as not to invalidate the dogma of Chalcedon.

May, therefore, the eastern brethren re-examine the subject touched upon here in the spirit of Christian brotherliness and love, and may they then revise their attitude to the Fourth Ecumenical Council and the Orthodox Catholic Church, especially since they claim that they reject the extreme Monophysitism of Eutyches, whom they personally condemn as did the great Council of Chalcedon, a Council which they falsely consider to be Nestorian in tendency. Thereafter it will be easy to settle the other secondary and unessential differences which exist between the divided churches in the spirit of love and of desire for understanding. Included among these secondary differences are the following: those with regard to the form of worship, those in connection with the canon, those regarding the number of ecumenical councils, and that resulting from the veneration rendered to Dioskoros, Patriarch of Alexandria, by some members of the eastern churches. In this connection, it is granted that he was not damned for heresy by the Fourth Ecumenical Council but was only deposed because of anti-canonical activities. As Anatolios, the Patriarch of Constantinople, stated in the fifth session of that Council: "Dioskoros was not deposed because of the faith, but because he excommunicated His Lordship Leo, the Archbishop, and, though summoned before the Council three times, did not appear (dia ten pistin ou katherethe ho Dioskoros, all' epeide akoinonesian epoiese to kyrio Leonti to archiepiskopo kai triton eklethe kai ouk elthen)" before the council.[34] What is more, the same Dioskoros expressly rejected the false teachings of Eutyches.[35]

---

[34] Mansi, *Sacrorum Conciliorum . . . collectio,* tom. 7, 104; Metropolitan of Nevrokopiou Georgios, *The Union of the Coptic with the Orthodox Church Is Easy* (Greek), (Saloniki, 1952), pp. 53/9.

[35] Mansi, *op. cit.,* tom. 6, 633. Schwartz, *op. cit.,* tom. II, 1, 92. 168.

Unification on the Basis of Cyril's Formula 43

DISCUSSION: Concerning the Paper of Professor Karmiris

FATHER SAMUEL: In the main your position is fully acceptable to Severus. There might be one or two points of detail that I would refer to later. If this is the position of the Eastern Chalcedonians, then we are in complete agreement.

ABBA HABTEMARIAM: I agree with these sentiments of Fr. Samuel. Yet there seems to be some difficulty about the nature of the union." I would like to know what is really the difficulty for you in speaking about *mia physis* after the union of two natures.

PROFESSOR KARMIRIS: We can speak of *one physis* after the union, but with the meaning of one *hypostasis*, with the four Chalcedonian qualifying adverbs: *asygchytos, atreptos, adiairetos, achoristos*.

ARCHBISHOP SEVERIUS: From our discussion so far I come to feel that there are no insoluble problems of doctrine between us concerning the Incarnation of our Lord Jesus Christ. We affirm that our Lord Jesus Christ is perfect God and perfect man, and that He is one Person and one nature. You also maintain the same faith by affirming that He is "in two natures." Whereas we emphasize the union of the natures, you insist on their distinctness.

We were afraid that the faith formulated by the Council of Chalcedon tended towards Nestorianism, and you were led by the misunderstanding that we were holding the heresy of Eutyches. However, the fact is that we are not Eutychians; neither are you Nestorians. Therefore, the way is clear before us for mutual understanding. This means that we have been, and still are, fighting about words and phrases.

We have all along been led by the feeling that there was enough ground at the Council of Chalcedon to justify our understanding that it favoured Nestorianism. But we see now that you understand the Council in a very different way, and that you exclude Nestorianism completely.

The fact that our difference is merely terminological was stated by one of our Church fathers, Gregory Bar Hebraeus of the thirteenth century, who was a man admirably conversant with the Greek language. "I am convinced," he said, "that the dispute of Christians among themselves is not based on essentials, but on words and terms. For all Christians confess that Christ our Lord is perfect God and perfect man without mixture and confusion of the natures. While one refers to the union (of the natures) as 'nature,' another calls it 'person' and a third 'prosopon.' Thus I see that all Christian people, though they remain separate, are, in fact, in agreement."

I am indeed most happy that this statement of Bar Hebraeus has been shown to be true to facts by our Consultation here.

PROFESSOR KARMIRIS: I have read the texts on both sides of the dispute. (a) I have come to the conclusion that there is no real difference between the Orthodox and the non-Chalcedonians as far as the essence of the Christological dogma is concerned, as all of them accept the teaching of St. Cyril of Alexandria. There is a difference only regarding the terminology and formulation of this dogma. In the same way there are secondary differences regarding worship, canon law, customs and uses, etc. But none of these things should divide the Churches; Photius, Patriarch of Constantinople, wrote: "Where matters of faith are not denied and there is no case of falling away from the common and catholic teaching accepted by all, when some maintain different customs and uses, one should not condemn those who profess or accept them. . . ."

(b) The Fourth Ecumenical Council must be understood and interpreted in the light of the teaching of the Third Ecumenical Council, as well as of the Fifth which is more directly related to it, because between these three Councils there is an agreement, continuity and unity completed by the Sixth Ecumenical Council. The Fourth Ecumenical Council should be understood also in the light of the teaching of St. Cyril of Alexandria, on which it is principally based.

(c) The theologians who participated in this Consultation should suggest to their Churches the appointment of a mixed commission of Orthodox and non-Chalcedonian theologians to determine and study deeply all the points of agreement and disagreement on the Christological dogma, as well as on subjects regarding worship, church administration, etc. This Commission should draft a *formulam concordiae* on the Christological dogma on the basis of the teaching of St. Cyril of Alexandria and of the other ancient Church Fathers and submit it in due time to their churches. The appointment of this Commission must be discussed and decided by the Third Pan-Orthodox Consultation which is to take place in Rhodes during this coming November, and by the Consultation which is to take place in Addis Ababa in the near future. The decisions and the actions to be taken afterwards depend entirely upon the Synods of the churches concerned, which should promote further and in a canonical way the sacred cause of the reunion of their churches.

ARCHBISHOP TIRAN: I was glad to listen to Professor Karmiris. But I would request our Greek brethren to stop saying that the non-Chalcedonian Fathers of the Church did not understand the terms used during the Christological controversy. The misunderstandings were due to the imprecise use of the Greek terms by the Greeks themselves, and not to the inadequacy of the other languages. The Catholicos-Patriarch Nersess IV of Armenia, who negotiated for union with the Emperor and Patriarch of Constantinople during the seventies of the 12th century, states that the difference beween the positions of the two sides is terminological and Chalcedonians and non-Chalcedonians are trying to express the same truth and the same orthodoxy. The realization of this fact did not help much to produce agreement, because there were many non-theological and sometimes non-essential elements which occupied the minds of people on both sides. However, we must thank God, the ground has now been cleared of these non-essential impediments and our task has thus been made easier.

PROFESSOR KARMIRIS: I agree with you. The problem of language is not a real one.

PROFESSOR MEYENDORFF: Our consultation seems to have reached a point where a common agreement seems to arise. This will probably become more obvious as the other papers are read.

Unification on the Basis of Cyril's Formula 45

If our difference is mainly terminological, then why were we separated for so many centuries? There may be something in the historical and cultural context which we need to clarify by investigation.

Our ecclesiologies are also identical. We do not insist on a single jurisdictional authority for the unity of the Church. The political unity of the Empire, a Roman idea, was however a dominant force in the early Byzantine history. It does not exist any more today, and no one should therefore be afraid of losing his independence.

We will have to find some kind of agreement in faith, but also a common approach to the historical background.

PROFESSOR ROMANIDES: The dogmatic continuity of both the Chalcedonian and non-Chalcedonian traditions through the Councils of Ephesus, 449, and Chalcedon, 451, can be seen in the fact that Dioscoros was considered quite Orthodox in his faith by such leading Fathers of the Council of Chalcedon as those represented by Anatolius of Constantinople. It is also significant that the Egyptian bishops asked to be temporarily exempt from signing the definition of Chalcedon on the grounds that they now, after the deposition of Dioscoros, had no Archbishop, and so could not act on the basis of the traditions of Egypt. They were cirticized by some for placing a local synod above an imperial ecumenical synod. This discussion concerning the relationship between local and ecumenical synods demonstrates clearly that the ecumenical synods convened by the Roman Emperors were imperial in nature and had the character of a pan-imperial ecclesiastical senate gathered in order to inform the government about the faith and practice of the Church for purposes of incorporating Church teaching and practice into the legal and social structures of the Roman Ecumene. The Nature of these imperial synods was demonstrated very vividly by the fact that at the tenth session of Chalcedon, when the bishops had reached a point wherein the Ephesine Synod of 449 was becoming aggravatingly problematical in dealing with the case of Ibas of Edessa, the bishops moved that a request be made to the emperor that the 449 Synod be erased from the lists of Ecumenical Synods. This clearly proves that the decisions of 449 were considered politically and ecclesiastically binding. Until this point in the deliberations at Chalcedon some of the acts of Ephesus 449 were reversed by dealing with them one by one, and other acts were simply accepted, as for example the decisions concerning Theodoret and Ibas who at Chalcedon were restored only when they anathematized Nestorius and accepted Cyril's *Twelve Chapters*. Therefore, not much attention was given to Leo of Rome's ravings over the heretical nature of this Dioscorian Synod. Besides indicating the ecclesiastico-political nature of the Ecumenical Synods, the aforementioned facts prove that the Council of Ephesus of 449 was not rejected for doctrinal reasons, especially since in this regard it simply repeated what was done at Ephesus I in 431. In the light of all this, first priority should be given in our discussions to whether or not the dogmatic decisions of individual synods are orthodox and not to whether or not the synods themselves are ecumenical. In a real sense even local synods are in nature ecumenical when the Orthodox faith is clearly proclaimed. One cannot fail to notice that Orthodox canon law makes frequent and precise provisions about the nature and function of local synods, but no references to the canonical structure and function of an ecumenical synod which was extraordinary in nature and beyond the normal synodical system of the Church's life and teaching authority.

BISHOP SARKISSIAN: Would a new formula expressing our common understanding of Christology solve the problem? Would such a formula alone be considered as a sufficient basis for restoring our communion in faith? And, then, how do we deal with the other problems which sometimes are described as "minor"? I refer particularly to the problem of the Council of Chalcedon as such and to the later three councils considered Ecumenical by the Byzantine Orthodox Church.

PROFESSOR KARMIRIS: Only one tradition should be taken into account — the dogmatic one. All the other points should be subsidiary to the dogmatic tradition. This latter is common to both of us. Therefore, we must consider this sufficient for our union. No primacies of Patriarchs and Bishops need be discussed nor are we interested in changing the polity of the churches. Only in certain words and definitions do we disagree. It is sufficient to recall the difference between St. Cyril of Alexandria and John of Antioch, who differed in their formulation, without any real difference in their faith.

BISHOP EMILIANOS: But harmony of dogma may not be adequate. Are there any other doctrinal differences arising out of the other Councils?

PROFESSOR KARMIRIS: Chalcedon adopted above all the teaching of St. Cyril. The synod did not base itself on the Tome of Leo. The Tome of Leo is a piece of paper among many materials in the Council. Papal delegates asked for its adoption as definition but the Eastern fathers refused. Egyptians, Palestinians, Illyrians, all refused, including the bishops of Illyricum who were under the jurisdiction of Leo. We have our own fathers who are the true teachers of the faith.

There are no differences between the Councils of 431 and 451 in dogma. So also there is no difference between all seven Ecumenical Councils. The faith is one and the same in all the councils. All came out of the same common tradition of the first centuries. There is a continuity and unity of faith among the Seven Councils. So there are no outstanding problems between us, whether we accept three or seven.

The differences in liturgical forms, canon law, customs and practical issues, as well as in the names of certain fathers of the Church venerated by different churches, need not be a problem. These do not separate; the precise formulation of the Christological dogma is the only thing that needs to be done.

ARCHBISHOP TIRAN: Nationalism in the sense in which we understand it now may not have existed in the 5th and 6th centuries. Still, there was exploitation and domination of class by class, or ethnic group by ethnic group. There were peoples which were different from each other and were opposed to each other. There were territorial loyalties or oppositions. Syrian, Egyptian, Armenian social entities resisted the centralism of the Empire. These tensions, called by whatever name, played a large part in the quarrels touched off by the turn of events connected with the Council of 451.

I would also like to make a remark on the attitude of the Egyptian bishops in the Council. Their refusal to sign the definitions of the Council has ecclesiological significance. They did not consider themselves as independent individual bishops free to accept or reject the decisions. They thought of themselves as a corpus of Bishops under their head, the Pope of Alexandria. They considered themselves as representing a distinct national-territorial Church within the Church of Christ universal. They did not feel that they could act without their archbishop. It is perhaps this ecclesiological concept that developed into self-governing national churches of modern times. We could perhaps call this concept the collegiality of the bishops of a national church.

PROFESSOR ROMANIDES: But we must keep in mind that among the Greek speaking Orthodox there is no one national Church, but rather six autocephalous Churches and two semi-autonomous Churches. Constantinople, Alexandria, Jerusalem, Cyprus, Greece, Sinai, Crete, and the Dodecanese. The many provincial synods of the Roman Empire were already autonomous or autocephalous. In the ancient Church, as with the Greeks today, synodical autocephaly had nothing essential to do with national or ethnic identity. The same can be said about the Latin synods of the West before the German invasions. Italy, for example, had at least two autocephalous groupings of bishops with centers in Rome and Milan. When the Church of Russia became autocephalous at the end of the 16th century, the Orthodox of the Ukraine remained under the jurisdiction of Constantinople till the rise of the modern Orthodox idea of identity of nationality and autocephaly.

PROFESSOR KARMIRIS: The Orthodox Church has one basis of unity, formulated by Photius of Constantinople. "Whenever that which is violated is not the faith, nor there is a fall from the common and catholic decree, because other customs and laws are kept by others, he who knows how to judge rightly should not think that they who keep these fall into *adikia* or that they who do not accept them violate the law." Cultural differences need not divide the Church.

PROFESSOR SAMUEL: I should like to refer here to two minor points of difference between the paper of Professor Karmiris and the position of Severus of Antioch. For Severus, the word "nature" in both the phrases "from two natures" and "one incarnate nature" means *hypostasis*. But he makes it clear that, while taking the word "nature" in this sense, he excludes two possible erroneous interpretations. Thus, in the first place he rejects "two natures before the union," which he thinks is Eutychianism. Secondly, he renounces the idea of two conjoint natures, which for him is Nestorian *synapheia*. He then interprets the "from two natures" in this way. God the Son, an eternal nature or *Hypostasis,* when He became incarnate, individuated manhood in a hypostatic union with Himself. Therefore, the union was "from two natures," namely the eternal *hypostasis* of God the Son and manhood which was individuated in that union. In the union the natures converged into one *hypostasis,* and thus Christ is always "one incarnate nature or *hypostasis* of God the Word," or He is "one composite (*synthetos*) nature." Severus opposed the Chalcedonian phrase "in two natures" on the argument that it would imply only the idea of the

Nestorian *synapheia*. But he rejected with equal force the idea that Christ was "one ousia." In his view, it was not simply human nature that God the Son assumed, but a full individuated manhood. In spite of this terminological difference, we can see here agreement in the essence of the faith.

I was glad to hear Professor Karmiris say that conciliar decisions are permanently binding only when these decisions are dogmatic, not about non-dogmatic matters. This has many implications.

PROFESSOR FLOROVSKY: I should like to be an *advocatus diabolus* because I feel the need. First I am wholeheartedly in favour of a reconciliation between Eastern Churches, but I am not for over-emphasis on the East. Eastern ecumenism is a contradiction in terms. The West also belongs to the oikoumene. We cannot afford to forget the West — and the Tome of Leo. The Christian tradition is universal. The Byzantine Church was afraid of precipitating a schism by rejecting Leo. We must also be careful.

We must not over-emphasize confessional formulae and a direct intellectual approach. In practice we have to discuss the difficulties of plurality of practice, and the problems of psychological attitudes. Can we say that jurisdiction is not a problem for unity? That we need not have some central symbol of unity? Question of authority is important. Who can coordinate the various local or national churches? Who will prepare this confessional formula on behalf of the churches? We have to have a full meeting of the bishops on both sides. Who will convene this?

I have also doubts about agreement on the basis of a one-sided Cyrillian formula. I think it is important to come to terms with the later ecumenical councils.

PROFESSOR KARMIRIS: Professor Florovsky is right in speaking about authority. But glory be to God, all the Eastern churches have the synodical system, the competent organs of each church, with a presiding Bishop, Patriarch or Metropolitan. The question must first be discussed in all of these local synods. The text would have to be drafted by a working group and presented to all the synods of the churches. We can discuss this at Addis Ababa next January and at Rhodes in November. After discussion in two meetings it can be sent again to the churches for final ratification. Finally, all the bishops can come together in Council to finalize the decision. This is our Eastern synodical system of making decisions.

We should not have in mind the example of certain theologians or get bogged down in discussions of primacy and so on.

PROFESSOR NISSIOTIS: Inspired by our agreement, I would go further to say:

Something fundamental is revealed when we meet together. The dogmatic discussion is not an isolated piece. We both share in the dogmatic continuity of the churches. Our agreement is in the life of our churches, Christology — ecclesiology — anthropology are inseparable. And we have on both sides preserved this one tradition in its entirety; we are one in the whole of dogma — not just in one point. What is behind all this is the very profound understanding of the Holy Spirit in the Church. We have to make evident this common agreement in Pneumatology to the whole oikoumene. The synodical system is not just a practical matter. It is the expression of our Christology and Pneumatology, our Eucharistic theology.

PROFESSOR SAMUEL: This is precisely why we consider ourselves Orthodox — not for prestige.

PROFESSOR KARMIRIS: St. John Damascene very clearly calls the non-Chalcedonians Orthodox in all matters with the exception of speaking of one *physis* after the union but not in the monophysite sense of one essence (*ousia*).

DR. KHELLA: The tragedy of Chalcedon is this: it had no formal conclusion as Ephesus 431. Our situation now is the same as, say, 432. If the reunion of 433 had not taken place, the 431 situation, that is the schism between Alexandria and Antioch, would have continued till now. But 451 did not come to a reunion formula.

In the period between 433 and 451 Cyril of Alexandria, John of Antioch and Proclus of Constantinople, the fathers and defenders of the union of 433, died. Their followers Dioscorus in Alexandria, Domnus in Antioch and Flavian in Constantinople did not trust each other. They brought the situation back to 432, as it was before the agreement of 433. It is very important to notice here that Leo of Rome was completely excluded from the discussion in the East: his later Tome was practically an arbitrary interference in matters which did not concern him.

One point which I like to emphasize in consideration of the paper of Professor Karmiris is that "*en duo physesin*" has no Greek tradition at all. It is surprising to find this coming out of Chalcedon. Chalcedonians would agree with us that "*ek duo physeon*" is the more traditional formula. It is rather surprising that the Greek Church accepted this formula presented by Leo of Rome. Leo had little comprehension of the theological issue behind the two prepositions. Let us judge the issue on the basis of the Acts of the Council of 451, which seems to reject the *ek* in favour of *en*, after having almost accepted *ek*.

Our Church accepts all Greek Fathers up to Chalcedon, but then none of them spoke of two natures after the union. We do not need to spend time discussing the Christology of Eutyches; both sides reject him. In fact, he was not a qualified theologian though politically rather important. Eutyches was a monk; his asceticism demanded the disparagement of the body; Christ's flesh would be consumed by His spirit or by the power of the Logos.

Today we can rediscover our joint tradition and testimony which were interrupted for fifteen centuries. But 1500 years of separation need not become an insurmountable barrier. We have today the possibility of finding our common way to the expression of our unity.

ST. CYRIL'S "ONE PHYSIS OR HYPOSTASIS OF GOD THE LOGOS INCARNATE" AND CHALCEDON[1]

THE VERY REV. PROF. JOHN S. ROMANIDES

Both Chalcedonian and non-Chalcedonian Orthodox accept St. Cyril as the chief Patristic exponent of Orthodox Christology. Yet both accuse each other of not remaining completely faithful to Cyril.

The non-Chalcedonian Orthodox reject the Council of Chalcedon and accuse it of Nestorianism because it accepted the *Tome of Leo, two natures after the union,* and allegedly omitted from its definition of faith such Cyrillian expressions as *One Nature of God the Logos Incarnate, hypostatic or natural union,* and *from two natures* or *from two One Christ.* The failure of Chalcedon to make full use of Cyril's *Twelve Chapters,* to condemn the Christology of *Theodore,* and its acceptance of *Theodoret* and *Ibas* throws suspicion on it. Then there is the weighty accusation that the very act of composing a new definition of the faith contradicted the decision of Ephesus (431) which decreed that, "It is unlawful for anyone to bring forward or to write or to compose another Creed besides that determined by the Holy Fathers assembled with the Holy Spirit in Nicaea."[2]

The Chalcedonian Orthodox, on the other hand, believe that it was Cyril's Christology which was not only fully accepted at Ephesus, but served as the basis of all judgments concerning Christology at Chalcedon in 451 and especially at Constantinople in 553. In spite of its obvious deficiencies the *Tome of Leo* is adequately Orthodox, definitely not Nestorian, and was accepted only as a document against Eutyches, but again only in the light of and in subordination to the synodical letters (especially the *Twelve Chapters*) of Cyril to Nestorius and John of Antioch, as we shall see. The terminology and faith of Cyril were fully accepted, although the Eutychian heresy, the chief concern of the Council,

---

[1] This paper presupposes familiarity with the article mentioned in note 4, p. 85.

[2] *Mansi,* IV, 1361.

called for some adaptation to the new situation. One may point out that the acceptance of the Chalcedonian definition was no different from the acceptance of Cyril's letters at Ephesus. Neither the one act nor the other can be considered as a composition of a new Creed. They are both interpretations and clarifications of the Nicaean faith in the light of modern circumstances. It is noteworthy that even Cyril had to defend himself against the accusation that he accepted a new Creed in his reconciliatory correspondence with John of Antioch.[3] Theodoret and Ibas were restored to the episcopacy because they accepted Ephesus I and especially the *Twelve Chapters*, which acceptance is in itself a condemnation of what they had written about and against Cyril and his anathemas. The Fifth Ecumenical Council of 553 anathematized the writings of Theodoret and Ibas against Cyril and the very person of Theodore, the Father of Nestorianism.

The non-Chalcedonian Orthodox have been for centuries accusing the Chalcedonian Orthodox of being Nestorians. On the other hand, the Chalcedonians have been accusing the non-Chalcedonians of either being monophysites (which for them means believers in *one ousia* in Christ) or of a one-sided insistence on Cyrillian terminology to the exclusion of Cyril's own acceptance of two natures in the confession of faith of John of Antioch which brought about the reconciliation of 433. This one-sidedness was adopted by the Ephesine Council of 449 and rejected by the Council of Chalcedon. It should also be noted that the Flavian Endemousa Synod of 448 was one-sided in its use of and insistence on the Cyrillian terminology of the 433 reconciliation to the near exclusion of Cyril's normal way of speaking about the incarnation. From Chalcedon and especially from Constantinople II it is clear that the Chalcedonians without compromise allow for variations in terms which express the same faith. On the non-Chalcedonian side Severus of Antioch seems to be the only one who comes close to Cyril's acceptance of *two natures tei theoriai monei* after the union, a position adopted at Chalcedon and clearly stated in the definition or anathemas of the Fifth Ecumenical Council.

The purpose of this paper is to discuss a few terms against the historical background of circumstances which called them up to serve as a test of correct faith. Especially important are the circumstances surrounding the Councils of 449 and 451. Undoubtedly

---

[3] *P.G.*, 77, 188.

a key figure which conditioned Dioscoros' exasperation with all talk of two natures was its extremely clever use by Theodoret to hide what one may call a clear case of crypto-Nestorianism. Leo's support of and failure to see through Theodoret made him guilty by association, as in some measure happened with Dioscoros' support of Eutyches. This explains a good deal of the negative attitude toward Leo's tome, not only from Egyptian quarters, but also from the Palestinian and, of all people, the Illyrian bishops, who were within Leo's own sphere of ecclesiastical influence.

The key to the approach of this paper is (1) to define Nestorianism as seen by Cyril in order to determine why Cyril could accept *tei theoriai monei* two natures in Christ after the union and John's confession of faith, and then (2) to examine very briefly in the light of this definition Leo's Tome and the attitude toward and use of it by Chalcedon. In Part II we will examine what is clearly a case of crypto-Nestorianism in the person of Theodoret, and in the light of this we will survey some of the important aspects of the Chalcedonian and non-Chalcedonian encounter with this issue. Throughout the paper we will be concerned with the place of Cyril, and especially his *Twelve Chapters,* at Chalcedon, thereby determining whether or not the Fifth Ecumenical Council is really a return to or rather a remaining with Cyril.

Part I

1) Nestorius rejected the fact that He Who was born of the Virgin is consubstantial with the Father according to divinity and thus by nature God. Another way of saying this is that he rejected the fact that He Who before the ages is born from and is consubstantial with the Father was in the last days born according to His Own and proper humanity from the Virgin Mary having become thus by nature man and consubstantial with us. On the basis of this rejection Nestorius distorted the true significance of the title *Theotokos* which he in reality denied to the Mother of God. The most Nestorius could say is that Christ is the one person of the union of two natures, the one nature being by nature God and the other by nature man. The name Christ is not properly predicated of the Logos, but is the name of the person of union born of Mary and in whom the Logos dwells and who was assumed by the Logos. Nestorius fanatically insisted that the Logos was not born of the Virgin according to His Humanity and did not, therefore, become by nature man. On the basis of this he

divided the natures and predicates of Christ attributing the human to the assumed man and the divine to the Logos.

In the light of his denial of the two births of the Logos and the double consubstantiality of the One and the Same Logos, Son of God and the Self-Same also Son of Mary, and thus of the true meaning of the title Theotokos, Nestorius' insistence that he does not divide Christ into two persons, but only the natures and names, was judged a mockery of the faith and on this basis he was condemned by the Third and Fourth Ecumenical Councils and rejected by John of Antioch and Leo of Rome.

I have indicated elsewhere[4] that the reconciliation of 433 between Cyril and John was brought about by the Antiochene's confession of the double birth and consubstantiality of "our Lord Jesus Christ, the Only-begotten Son of God," the very doctrine rejected so violently by Nestorius and even by Theodoret, as we shall see shortly. In his confession John clearly declares that the *Only-begotten Son of God* was "before the ages begotten from the Father according to His Divinity, and in the last days the *Self-same* (ton auton) for us and for our salvation, (begotten) of Mary the Virgin according to His Humanity, the Self-same (ton auton — note that he is here speaking clearly about the Only-begotten Son and not the Nestorian and Theodoretan Prosopon of the union of two natures) consubstantial with the Father according to Divinity and consubstantial with us according to Humanity."[5] For Cyril this confession of faith meant that the title Theotokos and the incarnation were accepted in their full and true significance, in spite of the fact that John spoke of "a union *of two natures,* whereby we confess One Christ, One Son, One Lord."

In his letter to Acacius of Melitene[6] Cyril is quite emphatic about the fact that this Antiochene confession of the double birth and double consubstantiality of the One and the Same Logos cannot be suspected of Nestorianism since this is exactly what Nestorius denies.[7] To the objection that two natures after the union

---

[4] See my article, "Highlights in the Debate Over Theodore of Mopsuestia's Christology," in *The Greek Orthodox Theological Review,* vol. v, no. 2 (1959-60), pp. 157-161.

[5] *Mansi,* IV, 292.

[6] *P.G.,* 77, 184-201. See also *Ep. ad Eulogium, P.G.,* 77, 224-228; *Ep. ad Successum I and II, P.G.,* 77, 228-245.

[7] *P.G.,* 77, 189-192, 197.

means a predication of two separate kinds of names, divine and human, to two separate natures, Cyril replies that to divide names does not mean necessarily a division of natures, hypostases, or persons, since all names are predicated of the one Logos. The division of names is considered as a safeguard against Arians and Eunomians who by confusing them sought to demonstrate the creatureliness of the Logos and His inferiority to the Father. The names, and not the natures, are divided in order to distinguish the real difference of the natures or things out of which Christ is composed, and not to divide them, since they can be distinguished after the union in contemplation only.[8]

Of course Cyril prefers to speak of *One Nature or Hypostasis of God the Logos Incarnate and become man,* since this better safeguards the union and the attribution of all things pertaining to Christ to the Logos as the subject of *all* human and divine actions. For Cyril *Physis* means a concrete individual acting as subject in its own right and according to its own natural properties. Thus the One Nature of God the Logos Incarnate, having by His second birth appropriated to Himself a perfect, complete and real Manhood, has as His Own both the ousia and natural properties common to all men, whereby it is the Logos Himself Who is Christ and lives really and truly the life of man without any change whatsoever in his Divinity, having remained what He always was. To speak about two natures in Christ would be somewhat equivalent to a Chalcedonian speaking about two Hypostases in Christ. In this respect a Chalcedonian would accept and does accept everythng Cyril says but would use Cyril's *One Hypostasis of God the Logos Incarnate,* since for him *Physis* means *Ousia.*

The one very essential point which Cyril makes and which some day may be given adequate consideration by the non-Chalcedonian Orthodox is that whatever one's insistence on theological accuracy in expression may be, it is sheer caricature to accuse anyone of being Nestorian who accepts the double birth and double consubstantiality of the Logos as the basis for the title Theotokos, as well as for the predication of all human and divine attributes and energies to the Logos Who is the sole subject incarnate and acting, both according to His Divinity and His Own appropriated Manhood. This is what Theodore, Nestorius, and Theodoret de-

---

[8] *P.G.,* 77, 193-197.

nied and this is the essence of Orthodoxy. St. Cyril saw this clearly and it is our duty to place this at the centre of our discussions.

2) There is no doubt that Leo tended to separate or distinguish the acts of Christ in such a way that the two natures seem to be acting as separate subjects, a tendency explainable by what he imagined Eutyches was teaching and by his Latin formation wherein Greek Trinitarian terms used in Christology were not available to him. He so obviously failed to understand how the term *One Nature* was being used in the East, and especially during the Endemousa Synod of 448. This is why a non-Chalcedonian reading the Tome should read *ousia* upon coming across *natura*, since Leo was dealing with the information he had received that Eutyches denied Christ's consubstantiality with us. His expression of utter amazement that the judges did not severely censure Eutyches when making such a statement as, "I confess that our Lord was from two Natures before the Union, but after the Union I admit but one Nature," confirms the confusing of his own *natura* and the Greek *ousia* with *physis*. Then Eutyches' own confusion of the terms *ousia* and *physis* did not help the matter any.

Nevertheless, Leo is very clear in his acceptance of the anti-Nestorian standard of Orthodoxy accepted by Cyril. Leo declares clearly in his Tome that "the Self-same, who was the Only-begotten and Everlasting One of the Everlasting Parent, was born of the Holy Spirit and the Virgin Mary. And this birth in time takes away nothing from that divine and eternal birth, nor does it add anything to it...."[9]

The definition of Chalcedon is also clear in this respect. "Following, then, the holy Fathers, we all unanimously teach that our Lord Jesus Christ is to us One and the same Son, the Self-same of a rational soul and body; consubstantial with the Father according to the Godhead, the Self-same consubstantial with us according to the Manhood ... before the ages begotten of the Father according to the Godhead, but in the last days, the Self-same, for us and for our salvation (born) of Mary the Virgin Theotokos according to the Manhood...."[10]

Returning to Leo's Tome it is important to point out that at Chalcedon it was accepted only as a document against the heresy

---
[9] T. H. Bindley, *The Ecumenical Documents of the Faith* (London, 1950), p. 224.
[10] *Mansi*, VII, 116.

of Eutyches, in spite of the fact that both Leo and his legates believed it to be a good statement against Nestorius also. It is even more important to keep in mind that during its reading at Session II the three now famous Nestorian sounding passages were each one challenged as the document was being read. During each interruption it was attacked and defended by the use of parallel passages from Cyril.[11] After what must have been a somewhat stormy and long debate, bishop Atticos of Nikopolis in Old Epirus, Greece, made the motion that time out be taken to give the assembly the opportunity to carefully compare Leo's Tome with the *Twelve Chapters* of Cyril in order to make sure of what they were approving.[12] The imperial representatives chairing the meeting gave the bishops five days in which to do this and suggested the formation of a committee under the presidency of Anatolius, Patriarch of Constantinople.[13] The committee reported back at the fourth session, at the beginning of which the imperial and senatorial representatives declared the unswerving faith of the emperor in the expositions of Nicaea, Constantinople, and Ephesus with its approval of the "two canonical letters of Cyril," i.e., the Second and Third to Nestorius.[14] This profession of the imperial faith had been made also at the end of Session I,[15] and now in anticipation of the committee's report on the question of Leo's agreement with Cyril's *Twelve Chapters* it was repeated. The committee report[16] was included in the minutes in the form of a listing of the individual opinions of its members, all of whom expressed their belief that Leo's Tome agreed with Nicaea, Ephesus, and *the letter* of Cyril. Most of the bishops mentioned *the* (one) *letter* of Cyril,[17] which cannot be any other than the *Twelve Chapters* since this was the one the Illyrians and Palestinians were concerned about as is clear from the motion of the Illyrian Atticos which initiated the careful comparison of Leo's Tome with the letter of Cyril. Some of the members mentioned their belief that the Tome agreed with the *two letters* of Cyril, clearly referring to the ones of Ephesus mentioned as part of the imperial faith. It is ex-

---

[11] *Mansi*, VI, 972-973.
[12] *Mansi*, VI, 973.
[13] *Mansi*, VI, 973.
[14] *Mansi*, VII, 8.
[15] *Mansi*, VI, 937.
[16] *Mansi*, VII, 48.
[17] *Mansi*, VII, 36-45.

St. Cyril's "One Physis" and Chalcedon 57

tremely interesting to note that among the similar individual opinions given by the rest of the Assembly and recorded in the minutes is that of none other than Theodoret of Cyrus,[18] who claims that he finds the Tome of Leo in agreement with *the letters* of Cyril and the Council of Ephesus, certainly a tremendous leap from his position just before the Council. In the light of his strong hesitation at Session VIII to anathematize Nestorius, a hesitation which infuriated the assembly, one wonders about his sincerity, especially since he tried to defend his former acts by an exposition of how he never taught two Sons. He was interrupted by shouts of "Nestorian."[19]

The acceptance of Leo's Tome in the light of and in subordination to the letters of Cyril is also clearly contained in the Chalcedonian definition itself.[20] It is declared that the Council accepts the Synodical (the Third letter to Nestorius is titled synodical, or since this is in the plural it could be a reference to the two of Ephesus, which in the minutes are called canonical, plus the one to John) letters of Cyril to Nestorius and to those of the East, "and to which (epistles) it reasonably *adapted* the letter of Leo . . . (epistolas . . . hais kai ten epistolen tou Leontos . . . eikotos synermose . . .)." This is not a case of a balance between Cyril *and* Leo, as many scholars would have us believe. Leo became very sensitive about the doubts raised about his tome, and especially disturbed did he become over determined opposition in certain quarters like Palestine where Juvenal was deposed for accepting the Tome. In a letter to Julian of Cos (CXVII, 3) in which he shows much concern with accusations of heresy against himself, he writes that, ". . . if they think there is any doubt about our teaching, let them at least not reject the writings of such holy priests as Athanasius, Theophilus and Cyril of Alexandria, with whom our statement of the faith so completely harmonizes that anyone who professes consent to them disagrees in nothing with us." No one can doubt the sincerity with which Leo wanted to be in agreement with those Alexandrine Fathers, but his defense of Theodoret compromised him. In a letter to the now restored Bishop of Cyrus he chides Theodoret for the tardy way in which he anathematized Nestorius (CXX, 5), yet in his opening remarks

---

[18] *Mansi*, VII, 20.
[19] *Mansi*, VII, 188-192.
[20] *Mansi*, VII, 113.

of this very same letter he speaks of "the victory you [Theodoret] and we together had won by assistance from on high over the blasphemy of Nestorius, as well as over the madness of Eutyches." Dioscoros' relationship to Eutyches may have some parallels.

The Chalcedonian definiton also speaks of itself as "preserving the order and *all* the decrees concerning the Faith passed by the Holy Synod held formerly at Ephesus. . . ."[21] From Ibas' *ad Marim Persam* and from the minutes of the Johannine Council of Ephesus, we learn that the Antiochenes rejected the Cyrillian Council of Ephesus and damned Cyril because the heretical *Twelve Chapters* had been accepted.[22] In this same letter Ibas (as were many of Cyril's friends and Theodoret)[23] was under the impression that Cyril abandoned his Ephesine position in his reconciliation with John in 433.[24] However, Ibas stated at his trial in Byretus in 449 that Paul of Emessa had accepted the Alexandrine bishop's interpretation of the *Twelve Chapters* as Cyril had accepted the confession of the Easterners.[25] It is in the light of this that one should read the letter of John to the bishops of Rome, Alexandria, and Constantinople (the order of the letter) in which he announces Antioch's acceptance of Nestorius' excommunication and the Council of Ephesus.[26] It is impossible to accept the opinion of many that Cyril laid aside his *Twelve Chapters* for the sake of a reconciliation with John. As an individual he had no authority whatsoever to modify the decisions of an Ecumenical Council and there is no evidence to substantiate this supposition. Although the Endemousa Synod of Constantinople seems to have overemphasized the Cyrillian allowances of 433, it accepted the *Twelve Chapters* as part of Ephesus which it approved *in toto*.[27]

In the light of the evidence it is clear that Cyril's Third letter to Nestorius, including the *Twelve Chapters*, was not repudiated by Chalcedon as many claim. On the contrary, the *Twelve Chapters* were used as the very basis of the Council's attitudes toward Nestorianism and Leo's Tome. It is too bad that the Chalcedonians themselves present at the Council of 531 in Constantinople

---

[21] *Mansi*, VII, 109.
[22] *Mansi*, IV, 1265 ff.; VII, 244-245.
[23] *Ep. CLXXI, P.G.*, 83, 1484.
[24] *Mansi*, VII, 248.
[25] *Mansi*, VII, 240.
[26] *Mansi*, V, 285.
[27] *Mansi*, VI, 665.

did not fully realize the crucial role played at Chalcedon by Cyril's *Twelve Chapters*. Their answer to Severus' accusation that the *Twelve Chapters* were laid aside in 451 was that it was accepted and approved as part of Ephesus I. This, of course, is incontestable, but not anywhere near the reality of the matter. The significance of the use made of the *Twelve Chapters* at Chalcedon should be obvious enough to those who claim that they fail to find the terms characteristic of Cyrillian Christology in the definition. Groundless also are the theories (brought forward by many Protestant and Roman Catholic scholars embarrassed by the Cyrillianism of the Fifth Ecumenical Council) concerning an alleged neo-Chalcedonian movement which was supposed to have put Leo's Tome aside and returned to the *Twelve Chapters* of Ephesus I, especially to the *twelfth anathema*. The truth of the matter is that in pronouncing anathema on those who do not accept the *Twelve Chaptres* of Cyril, the Fifth Ecumenical Council of 553 is simply repeating what was done at Ephesus in 431 and again at Chalcedon in 451.

Part II

Now we must turn to the crypto-Nestorianism of Theodoret, a type of Christology which in some measure can hide itself behind the language used in the formulary of reunion of 433, without, however, adopting its exact wording and meaning. It was undoubtedly his exasperation with this type of Antiochene Christology more than anything else which goaded Dioscoros into setting aside Cyril's act of 433 and returning to what may be called Alexandrine exclusiveness as the only sure means of uprooting the new form behind which Nestorianism hid itself.

In the course of the Christological controversies Theodoret learned to modify some of his opinions without, however, changing his basic vision and presuppositions. For example, he rejected Cyril's suggestion that the Logos Himself became by nature man,[28] but by the time he wrote his *Eranistes* he had adapted, to some degree, his language to that of Cyril. In some contrast to Nestorius he claims that "the Truth is both God by nature and man by nature."[29] In another work he says that "the Same is by nature God and man."[30] He Who was born of the Virgin, according to

---

[28] *Ep. De XII Capitulis*, P.G., 76, 388A.
[29] *P.G.*, 83, 121B.
[30] *Demonstrationes*, P.G., 83, 328A.

Theodoret, is consubstantial with the Father according to His Godhead and consubstantial with us according to His Manhood. Christ was born, says the bishop of Cyrus, before the ages from God the Father and in our own time the Selfsame Christ was born from the Virgin Theotokos.[31] These expressions are not those of Nestorius, yet they are not completely Orthodox. The name Christ, for Theodoret, is predicated of the Logos because the Only-begotten Son of God assumed a man or manhood which was born from the Virgin.[32] Until his acceptance of the Third and Fourth Ecumenical Councils, Theodoret could not say that the Logos Himself, being by nature God, became according to the flesh by nature man, or consubstantial with us, by His second birth in time from the Virgin Mary, while remaining immutably what He was. Such a double birth and the double consubstantiality must be predicated of Christ alone and not the Logos. Only divine names can be predicted of the Logos.[33] Yet all names, both human and divine, can be predicated of Christ because of the union in Him of the two natures.[34] Thus, when Theodoret says that He Who was born of the Virgin is consubstantial with God the Father, he does not mean that He Who is consubstantial with the Father was born of Mary in the flesh. The name Christ seems to be the only one Theodoret allows to be predicated of the Logos in the flesh, and by means of this he avoids saying with Nestorius that Christ is the Son of David and Son of God united in His (Christ's) One Person. Yet he clearly follows Nestorius by distinguishing the Only-begotten Son and Christ in the Creed by insisting that the name Jesus Christ, and not the title of Only-begotten Son, is the recipient of the things human such as birth, suffering, death, burial and resurrection.[35] His attempt to explain why only the name Christ of all things human should be predicated of the Logos in the flesh is a Nestorian failure. Thus it was the prosopon of Christ Who suffered, died, and was buried in the tomb, not the impassible Logos in His Own passible manhood.[36] When St. Paul speaks of the Lord of Glory being crucified he means that the body of the

---

[31] *P.G.*, 83, 1420.
[32] *P.G.*, 83, 264B; 280-281.
[33] *Ibid.*
[34] *P.G.*, 83, 148AB; 252CD; 231A.
[35] *P.G.*, 83, 280BCD-281B.
[36] *P.G.*, 83, 257CD; 261BCD.

Lord of Glory was crucified, not that the Lord of Glory was crucified in the flesh. [37]

Very instructive on the question of dividing the names between the two natures and uniting them, not in the Logos, but in the name Christ, which includes the Logos, is Theodoret's version of the formulary of reunion or Antiochene confession of faith. The linguistic variations between the confessions are doctrinally quite revealing. We will quote Theodoret's version[38] and insert in their proper places within brackets and in capitals the longer text of John and underline the one phrase in Theodoret's creed missing from that of John.

"We confess one Lord Jesus Christ, (THE ONLY-BEGOTTEN SON OF GOD), perfect God and perfect man, of rational soul and body, before the ages begotten of the Father according to Godhead, but in the last days (THE SELF-SAME) for us and our salvation, of Mary the Virgin; *the self-same* consubstantial with the Father according to Godhead, and consubstantial with us according to Manhood."

For John it is the Only-begotten Son of God Who has a double birth and a double consubstantiality, whereas for Theodoret these can be predicated only of Christ, Who includes the Logos, since only the single divine birth and consubstantiality can be predicated of the Logos Himself. It seems highly doubtful that Theodoret is the author of the formulary of reunion as is commonly claimed.[39] On occasion he may profess agreement with John' confession, but then he professed agreement with the Nicaean Creed also. On the basis of this crypto-Nestorianism Theodoret could continue his attacks on Ephesus and Cyril, and especially on the *Twelve Chapters*. It is very important to point out that Theodoret's Christology is not that of John accepted by Cyril, nor that of Leo's Tome and Chalcedon. Failure to realize this during the fifth century made both Leo and Chalcedon guilty by association

---

[37] *P.G.*, 83, 280AB.

[38] *Ep. CLI, P.G.*, 83, 1420A.

[39] Also doubtful on the basis of his Christology is Theodoret's alleged authorship of what seems to be a letter sent by Domnus to Flavian (*P.G.*, 83, 1297. See R. V. Sellers, *The Council of Chalcedon* (London, 1953), p. 28, n. 5) in which it is confessed that all things pertaining to Christ, although predicated of two natures, are attributed "to the One Only-Begotten."

in the eyes of those who followed the lead of Dioscoros, in the same way that Dioscoros was made guilty by association by his support of Eutyches.

Keeping in mind Theodoret's distinction between the titles Christ and the Only-begotten Son for the purpose of denying that the Nicaean Creed speaks of the Only-begotten Son Himself as born, suffering, crucified and buried, it is instructive to turn to Leo's Tome. The bishop of Rome, in clear contrast to Theodoret and Nestorius, writes, "that the Son of God is said to have been crucified and buried, although He suffered these things not in His Godhead itself, in virtue of which the Only-begotten is both co-eternal and consubstantial with the Father, but in the weakness of Human nature. And this is the reason why we all confess, too, in the Creed that 'the Only-begotten Son of God was crucified and buried' in accordance with that saying of the Apostle, 'For had they known they would not have crucified the Lord of Majesty' " (ch. 5). If this is not *in toto* what Cyril is saying in the *Twelfth Anathema* of his *Chapters*, it at least is certainly not what Nestorius or Theodoret were saying. In the opinion of this writer, Theodoret's acceptance of Leo's Tome in his need for help against personal disaster is no different from his acceptance of Cyril's *Twelve Chapters* at Chalcedon. He was a sorry sight at the eighth session trying to publicly convince the assembly that he was not now accepting all that was done and anathematizing Nestorius because of any love of honour, rank and wealth.[40]

As long as Cyril and John were alive they were able to contain somewhat the extremists in their respective dioceses (dioikeseis). Even the eruption of the controversy over the Christology of Diodore and Theodore did not break up the union of 433. However, things changed for the worse with the accession of Domnos (443) to the "Apostolic See" of Antioch and Dioscoros (444) to the "Evangelical See" (so they are called in the minutes of the Councils) of Alexandria. Theodoret got the upper hand in Antioch and pro-Nestorian activities increased seriously. Evidently at Theodoret's instigation several Nestorians were ordained bishops, including the notorious Nestorian fanatic Count Irenaeus the twice married. Thus the Church was faced with a resurgence of a Nestorianism hiding behind the formulary of reunion and Theodoretan Christological double-talk. Again we must keep in

---

[40] *Mansi*, VII, 188-192.

mind that these people not only professed faith in the formulary of reunion, but also in the Nicene Creed, both of which they interpreted in their own way.

At the time Cyril accepted John's confession there were many who were highly suspicious of the two nature document, either feeling that Cyril had compromised the decisions of Ephesus or believing that Cyril had been tricked. They no doubt felt that now their suspicions had been justified. It was now natural for them to feel and decide that the only way to uproot this new Nestorianism was to insist on *One Nature of God the Logos Incarnate, One Nature after the Union,* and that Christ is *One from or out of two Natures.* Only this would make it possible to insure the attribution of all the names and activities of Christ to the Logos Incarnate. The Theodoretan type experience had proven to them beyond all doubt that any doctrine of two natures after the union could only mean two subjects and centres of activity in Christ acting in a harmony of wills, the one or the other performing its proper operations as the need arose. As we shall see he assailed even those who could accept *One Nature of the Logos Incarnate,* but who preferred to speak of *two Physeis* which to them meant *two ousiai.*

The opportunity for a decisive blow at two natures was presented by the Endemousa Synod of Constantinople in 448 which was convened to deal with the accusation of heresy filed against Eutyches by Eusebius of Dorylaeum. The libel itself contains no specific heresy, but according to the witness of those sent to invite Eutyches to attend the Council in order to answer to unnamed charges, the aged Archimandrite denied that Christ is consubstantial with us according to manhood.[41] The same denial was repeated by Eutyches when he finally made a personal appearance at the Synod. However, when told that this is a denial of the teaching of the Fathers (perhaps some Patristic quotations were shown to him) he faltered and showed some willingness to accept this teaching. However, it is interesting to note that he was several times asked as one question what perhaps should have been asked as two separate questions, viz. whether or not he confesses (1) that Christ is consubstantial with us, and (2) that after the incarnation there are two natures in Christ.[42] There seem to be no indi-

---

[41] *Mansi*, VI, 700-701; 741.
[42] *Mansi*, VI, 737; 808; 816.

cations from the minutes (except possibly in Leo's observation that no one reprimanded the monk when he spoke of *One Nature* after the union) that these two statements could have different meanings, viz. that it may be possible to speak of One Nature of God the Logos Incarnate or one nature after the union, and at the same time confess that Christ is consubstantial with us according to His Manhood. Thus, although Eutyches could seriously entertain the possibility of accepting the teaching on consubstantiality, he could not for a moment think of anathematizing those who teach One Nature after the union. Thus when the two questions were thrown at him as one he could only refuse to anathematize. It seems quite clear that for Eutyches (whose case seems to be one of simple ignorance), as well as for Eusebius and Flavian, *physis* was synonymous with *ousia*. Eutyches was excommunicated, but either during the Synod or later he appealed his case to the bishops of Rome, Alexandria, Jerusalem, and Thessalonica.

Although Eutyches was quite defendable in his refusal to anathematize those who teach One Nature Incarnate of the Logos, since, as he said, he could not anathematize the Fathers of the Church, he could not be defended for his denial that Christ is consubstantial with us. Thus it was not after this Synod that Dioscoros accepted Eutyches into communion. This could not be done until the question of Christ's consubstantiality was cleared up. This doctrinal deficiency was done away with on the basis of added testimony presented to the Review Conferences of April 449 convened to examine Eutyches' claim that the acts of the Endymousa Synod which condemned him were inaccurate and lacking.

Presbyter John, who, together with the deacon Andrew (with another deacon, Athanasius, happening along), was sent to invite Eutyches to the Endemousa Synod, and had then testified that Eutyches denied that Christ is consubstantial with us, now claimed that in private, while the other two were not listening, the Archimandrite expressed his belief that *Christ is consubstantial with His mother,* although not with us.[43] When asked why this information was withheld in 448 Presbyter John answered that he had done this because the other two had not witnessed to this part of the conversation. The presbyter's testimony is peculiar since Eutyches did say that the mother of Christ was consubstantial with

---

[43] *Mansi*, VI, 785.

St. Cyril's "One Physis" and Chalcedon 65

us.[44] If he believed that Christ was consubstantial with his mother, this would, as it seems, make Him consubstantial with us also. It is interesting to note that Flavian himself uses the phrase that Christ is consubstantial with His mother in his confessions of faith.[45]

It is very important to realize that at this Review Conference it was established, truthfully or falsely, that Eutyches was excommunicated for refusing to anathematize those who say One Nature after the Union and for refusing to accept two natures after the Union. Constantine the deacon, one of Eutyches' advocates at the hearing, accused Flavian of doing just this.[46] The Patrician Florentius vigorously challenged the truthfulness of the acts which pictured him as attempting to get Eutyches to accept two natures after the union as though this only were Orthodox dogma.[47] There is also evidence indicating that on the basis of Cyril's *One Nature of God the Logos Incarnate* it was felt that Eutyches must agree with the bishops assembled.[48] This evidently meant that they felt Eutyches should accept a second nature in Christ since this is what to them *Incarnate* meant. Of course, this would be true if *Physis* meant *Ousia*, but this is not how Cyril used the term in this phrase. He could not and never does speak of *One Ousia of God the Logos Incarnate*. This paralleling of Cyril's *One Physis* with *Incarnate* in order to prove that Cyril speaks of *Two Physeis* in Christ was and is a mistake repeated by all Chalcedonians till today. The approach was and is a bad one since it could only lead to two *Hypostases* and *Prosopa*. Nevertheless, Eutyches was not restored to communion as a result of this Review Conference, either because Presbyter John's testimony was not accepted, or because Eutyches refused to accept two natures after the union.

What is of great significance from the foregoing is the fact that the Council of Ephesus of 449 was not heretical since Eutyches' exhoneration was obviously based on his confession that Christ is consubstantial with His mother. This explains why Anatolius of Constantinople at the Fourth Ecumenical Council could in plenary session claim that Dioscoros was not deposed

---

[44] *Mansi*, V, 1233; VI, 741.
[45] Sellers, *op. cit.*, pp. 130-131.
[46] *Mansi*, VI, 808; 816.
[47] *Mansi*, VI, 808-809.
[48] *Mansi*, VI, 813.

for heresy.[49] The Ephesine Council of 449 was rejected at Chalcedon because of the injustice done to Flavian and Eusebius, and the exhoneration of Eutyches. On the other hand Theodoret and Ibas, who were also deposed at Ephesus in 449, were restored at Chalcedon as late as sessions eight, nine, and ten, and then only after they accepted all that had thus far been done at the Council and anathematized Nestorius. Even though Leo's legates considered Theodoret as a participant from the very beginning,[50] the assembly vigorously protested.[51] The result of the protest can be seen in that the imperial representatives informed the protesting Dioscoros that the bishop of Cyrus was admitted to the Council in the capacity of accuser only.[52] We recounted his restoration elsewhere.[53] It should be noted that Atticos, the bishop of Nikopolis in Old Epirus, who made the motion which brought about the careful comparison of Leo's Tome with Cyril's *Twelve Chapters*, was present at Theodoret's restoration and the Epirot's acceptance of it is another testimony to the Bishop of Cyrus' submission to Cyril.[54]

Another objection, and perhaps the most serious, which Chalcedonian Orthodox have with the Ephesine Council of 449 is its rejection of Cyril's allowance for two natures after the union and its one-sided exclusiveness in this regard. This comes out clearly in the fact that at the Flavian Synod of 448 the minutes of Ephesus were read and accepted[55] and also by the fact that both Flavian and Eusebius accepted *One Nature of God the Logos Incarnate* so long as Christ's consubstantiality with us is clearly professed.[56] However, Dioscoros simply rejected all talk of two natures after the union. When the imperial representatives asked why Flavian was deposed since he did accept *One Nature of the Logos Incarnate*, Eustathius of Berytus admitted making a mistake.[57] Dioscoros, however, claimed that Flavian contradicted himself by accepting two natures after the union.[58] The strange thing is that both

---

[49] *Mansi*, VII, 104.
[50] *Mansi*, V, 589.
[51] *Mansi*, V, 592.
[52] *Mansi*, V, 644-645.
[53] *Mansi*, VII, 188-192. See remarks in text of this article at note 19, page 89 above.
[54] *Mansi*, VII, 188.
[55] *Mansi*, VI, 665.
[56] *Mansi*, VI, 637; 676-677.
[57] *Mansi*, VI, 677.
[58] *Mansi*, VI, 681.

were correct, since for Flavian *physis* meant *ousia*, whereas for Dioscoros it meant *hypostasis*. Nevertheless, knowingly or not Dioscoros was bent on erasing what Cyril had done in 433.

In confronting Eutyches' denial that Christ is consubstantial with us Flavian and Eusebius were clearly speaking of *two physeis* as equivalent to *two ousiai*. For them double *consubstantiality* meant *two natures*. For Eutyches *physis* and *ousia* were also synonymous and he evidently at first believed that Cyril's *One Nature* meant *One Ousia*, hence his hesitation to accept them as names for Christ's humanity. Cyril does use *ousia* and *physis* as synonymous when speaking of the Holy Trinity.[59] There is no question of course about his use of *physis* as equivalent to *hypostasis*. Yet he never speaks of there being *one ousia* in Christ and clearly speaks of the flesh of Christ as being consubstantial with ours.[60] In Christology he uses *physis, hypostasis,* and *prosopon* as synonymous, yet he never, as far as I know, speaks of *Two Prosopa before the union and one after,* as he does with the other two terms. Equivalent to his *One Nature of God the Logos Incarnate* is his *One Hypostasis of God the Logos Incarnate* of his *Third Letter to Nestorius*[61] and his *Defense of the Twelve Chapters.*[62] In the light of all this and all which was said at Chalcedon, the anathema pronounced in the definition on those who say *two natures before the union and one after the union* was intended for anyone with Eutyches who denied that Christ is consubstantial with us. There is no doubt that the definition should have contained the phrase *or ousia* as one finds after the phrase *one physis* in the eighth and ninth anathemas of the Fifth Ecumenical Council. This would have avoided much misunderstanding. It perhaps was not done at the Fourth because possibly Cyril's *One Nature of God the Logos* was taken as equivalent to *One Ousia* and the word *Incarnate* as equivalent to a *second ousia or physis*. That this was possible is borne out clearly by the Flavian Synod of 448, as well as the explanations given by both Eusebius and Flavian at Ephesus in 449, as we have already indicated.

It should be noted that *One Hypostasis of God the Logos Incarnate* and not *One Physis of God the Logos Incarnate* is to be

---

[59] E.g., *Ad Monachos, P.G.,* 77, 17.
[60] *Mansi,* VI, 677.
[61] *P.G.,* 77, 116.
[62] *Apologia Cap. II, P.G.,* 76, 401A.

found in Cyril's *Third Letter to Nestorius* approved by Ephesus and Chalcedon. These terms are, of course, absolutely synonymous for Cyril. Yet it seems very obvious that at the Flavian Synod of 448 and at Chalcedon, the true Cyrillian meaning or usage of *One Nature* was overlooked simply because the phrase *One Nature after the union* was not contained in the synodical letters of Cyril which alone were familiar to all participants of both Councils.

At the Endemousa Synod of Constantinople in 448[63] and in his confession of faith of 449 Flavian says that Christ is *out of or from two natures*.[64] Yet he spoke in the same breath of two natures after the union. At the Council of Chalcedon Dioscoros vigorously rejected any talk of a *union of two natures* (as found in the formulary of reunion approved by Cyril) and insisted exclusively on a *union out of or from two natures*. For Dioscoros this meant that after the union there could be only one nature. Had this term had the same function for Flavian as it did for Dioscoros, the bishop of New Rome would have found himself believing with Eutyches in *one ousia after the union,* since for him *physis* meant *ousia*. Nevertheless, the imperial representatives were so impressed by the fuss Dioscoros made over this question, that they used this as an example to convince the bishops of the need of drafting a statement of faith. It is at this point that Anatolius intervened to remind the assembly that Dioscoros was not deposed for heresy, but because he excommunicated Leo.[65] In their interlocution at the fifth session the imperial representatives said that Leo says *union of two natures* whereas Dioscoros says *union out of two natures*. "Whom do you follow?" they asked. The Reverend Bishops cried, "As Leo, thus we believe. Those who gainsay are Eutychinists."[66] In the light of what happened in sessions two and four with Leo's Tome, one wonders if a deliberate attempt was made with the minutes to make Leo look a little better at Chalcedon in order to offset the obvious humiliation he underwent. Keeping in mind the Council's subordination of Leo to Cyril one must take seriously the fact that in the letters of Cyril which served as the basis of the Council's deliberations the terms *from two natures* or *from two One* occur several times. It is understandable that Dioscoros made this a big issue and it so became sub-

---

[63] *Mansi*, VI, 680.
[64] Sellers, *op. cit.*, p. 131.
[65] *Mansi*, VII, 104.
[66] *Mansi*, VII, 105.

sequently. One can understand the imperial representatives trying to make the question look like a big victory for Leo. Attila had to be met by the force of an empire united in everything and especially helpful was the bishop of Rome who must not now be humiliated. But even when *in two natures* is accepted as the original reading of the Chalcedonian definition (although *from two natures* is what the manuscripts contain), it should be taken as an anti-Eutychianist statement meaning *in two ousiais*, since this is what had been denied. Thus the Fifth Ecumenical Council rejects as heretical *from two natures* only when its proponents mean to teach *one ousia* in Christ. It stands to reason that had anyone proposed *in two natures* in the sense of rejecting Cyril's *from two natures* he would have certainly been challenged. Anatolius' reply to the imperial representatives is indicative of the fact that the leaders of the Council were not in any mood to see in these phrases any contradiction, and in fact there were none. Would the non-Chalcedonian say that Christ is *out of two ousiai* in the same way he says *out of two physeis?* If not then he can't expect a Chalcedonian to do what he won't. What is then left is to speak of Christ as *of two ousiai* or *in two ousiais*. This is all a Chalcedonian means by *of two natures* and *in two natures*. It seems that bickering over such terms was the result of a heresy hunting temper which lumped Leo and Theodoret into one theological camp because of the alliance between them.

Also one may point out that *hypostatic union* or *natural union* were accepted at Chalcedon by virtue of the fact that all done at Ephesus in 431, the most important part of which are Cyril's letters wherein are contained all his key terms and ideas on Christology, was incorporated together with Cyril's letter to John and the Tome of Leo into the definition itself. It seems obvious enough that the Chalcedonian theologians of the fifth and sixth centuries should be taken very seriously when they point out that Chalcedon was not convened in order to condemn Nestorius, except by way of repeating what had been done so well at Ephesus in 431, but rather in order to deal with the Eutychianist heresy.

The Theodoretan crypto-Nestorianism, whose danger loomed so large in Alexandrian circles, was not at all grasped by Leo. In a similar fashion the danger of Eutychianism was not handled properly by Dioscoros. We must always keep in mind the serious imbalance of attitudes toward issues on each side. While the Chalcedonians concentrated on the *confusors of the ousiai* in

70 Does Chalcedon Divide or Unite?

Christ, the Alexandrians were still fighting the *separators of natures or hypostases*. In the light of this it would be wise to make allowances in terminology while none whatsoever in faith. I would suggest that serious consideration be given to the Fifth Ecumenical Council, not as one which modified Chalcedon, but as one which interprets it correctly. If we agree on the meaning of Cyril's Christology, we should also be as pliable as he on terms. In this regard the non-Chalcedonians should accept all of Cyril, including 433, and the Chalcedonians must stop overemphasizing the Cyril of 433.

DISCUSSION: Concerning the Paper of Father Romanides

FATHER MEYENDORFF: I am glad that Father Romanides speaks this time in this positive way about the Tome of Leo, and I hope the non-Chalcedonians will read him in this light. The praises of Leo in the Acts of Chalcedon should be seen as a conciliatory move in the light of the anti-Roman bias of the Chalcedonian Canons.

FATHER ROMANIDES: It is my opinion that the adoption of Trinitarian terms in Christology was in the beginning rather accidental. At the Council of Alexandria in 362, presided over by St. Athanasius the Great, it was decided to adopt the Cappadocian manner of distinguishing between *hypostasis* and *ousia* when speaking about the Holy Trinity. No decision was made concerning the term *physis* which, until the Cappadocian distinction came into existence, was synonymous for all practical purposes with both *hypostasis* and *ousia*. The outcome of this was that the Cappadocian tradition ended up by equating *physis* with *ousia*, while the Alexandrian tradition equated *physis* with *hypostasis*. The accidental nature of this equating of *physis* with either *hypostasis* or *ousia* must be taken seriously into consideration in order to understand the history of the Christological debates between 448 and 451 as described in my paper. In the self-justifying heat of polemics after 451 each side claimed a monopoly of understanding of the precise meaning of the term *physis* which from the point of view of the history of dogma is untenable. Failure to realize this can only lead us back to the ridiculous debate concerning the superiority of one's own Fathers over the Fathers of the other side. We must be very clear about the fact that the Chalcedonians mean two *ousiai* when they speak of two *physeis* after the union, whereas the non-Chalcedonians, as pointed out very clearly by Father Samuel's paper also, do not mean *one ousia* when they speak of *one physis* after the union.

FATHER MEYENDORFF: *Physis* was seen by all as signifying concrete being. The Antiochene Christology insisted upon the idea that the concrete actions of Christ can be variously ascribed to humanity and divinity, the subject being one — the Christ.

FATHER ROMANIDES: But Cyril would attribute everything to the Logos in the flesh, not simply to the Christ as is done by the Nestorianizers and pointed out in my paper.

FATHER VERGHESE: What do we mean by Christ being in two *ousiai* after the union?

FATHER ROMANIDES: In both the Cappadocian and Alexandrian traditions the *ousia* of God is beyond all categories of thought in a radical manner and therefore not only beyond definition of any kind, but also beyond the predication of any name whatsoever, to such an extent that God is *hyper-onymos, hyper-ousios* and even *hyper-theos*. Within this Biblical tradition the *ousia* of man also remains a mystery. Only the energies and powers of both God and man can be known. In this sense the term *ousia* is used not in the Greek philosophical sense of the definable and knowable immutable inner reality of a thing, but as concrete unknowable reality known only in its acts. In contrast to the Antiochene and Latin tradition (the Augustinian one), the term *ousia* as applied to the Holy Trinity by the Cappadocian and Alexandrian Fathers is neither a platonic superstratal genus, nor an Aristotelian substratal material in which the hypostases or persons of the Holy Trinity participate. Therefore, Christ being in *two ousiai* could only mean that our Lord, the Only-Begotten Son of God, exists in two concrete, yet undefinable and perfect and complete realities, each of which is by nature proper to Himself and distinguishable in the union in thought alone. The term *in two natures* is of Latin provenance and was translated by the Cappadocian oriented Fathers of Chalcedon by the phrase *in two physeis*. Under more normal conditions the Alexandrians might have accepted the term in their own theological language as *in two ousiai*. It is only in this anti-Eutychian sense that the non-Chalcedonians must understand the term *in two physeis* whose only intent is to preclude *one ousia* after the union.

FATHER SAMUEL: I am quite pleased with this paper of Father Romanides from several points of view. First, I am pleasantly surprised that Theodoret is not defended by the paper. Secondly, Ephesus (449) is not condemned outright. The paper is much fairer at this point than most Western church historians. Some difficulties remain for anyone reading the minutes of the Council. They do not give me the same impression as they give Father Romanides. Take, for instance, the Third Letter of Cyril to Nestorius with the Twelve Anathemas. At Chalcedon it was not read. The imperial commissioners referred to the two canonical letters of Cyril read and approved at Ephesus in 431. But the letters of Cyril read at Chalcedon were only his Second Letter to Nestorius and his Letter to John of Antioch, or the Formulary of Reunion of 433. So from the point of view of reading, the Third Letter with the Anathemas was passed over in silence. There were two references to it at Chalcedon. One: the intervention of Atticus of Nicopolis who wanted to compare the Tome of Leo with the Twelve Anathemas. And two, the Chalcedonian Formula includes it, by implication, among the documents of the Faith .

How, then, can Father Romanides say that the Twelve Chapters of Cyril were in the mind of the Council when it accepted the Tome of Leo?

FATHER ROMANIDES: Father Samuel is correct in saying that the *Third Letter* of St. Cyril to Nestorius containing the *Twelve Chapters* was at first passed over in silence. However, after the reading of Leo's *Tome* the successful demand was made that it be compared with the *Twelve Chapters* of St. Cyril in order to see whether or not it was Orthodox. We should not overlook the fact that the overwhelming majority of bishops at Chalcedon were Cyrillians and so were able to force the issue of the *Twelve Chapters* as the criterion of Leo's faith. After Chalcedon even Leo attempted to calm his enemies with the claim that he himself was absolutely Cyrillian (see e.g. his Ep. CXVII, 3). I think one should simply check the references to the minutes in my paper for documentation of the evaluations made.

FATHER SAMUEL: I am glad to hear you say that the Twelve Chapters were accepted by Chalcedon, though this is far from clear in the minutes.

In the matter of Ibas, for instance, the Roman delegates said that they had read his letter to Maris the Persian and that in spite of it they considered him Orthodox.

FATHER ROMANIDES: But Ibas was reinstated on the basis of his formal acceptance, sincere or not, of the Twelve Chapters.

FATHER SAMUEL: Besides, if I may continue, there is no basis for the statement that Dioscorus accepted Eutyches into communion if by this a serious charge is intended to be made against Dioscorus. There are several difficulties here. In the first place, we have to clarify the meaning of the word "communion" or *koinonia*. It can mean either Eucharistic communion or simply friendship and support. What is to be proved, if it can be raised as a charge, is that between the Home Synod of Constantinople in 448 and the second Council of Ephesus in 449 Dioscorus offered Eutyches Eucharistic communion. Do we have any evidence for it? Secondly, in none of the petitions against Dioscorus presented to the Council of Chalcedon was this mentioned. The only reference to it is found in the declaration against Dioscorus made by the Roman delegation. They said that Dioscorus had offered *koinonia* to Eutyches before the latter was rehabilitated at Ephesus in 449, without specifying what they meant by the word *koinonia*. Thirdly, while stating why Dioscorus had been condemned, Anatolius of Constantinople did not mention this as a charge against Dioscorus. Thus if at all one has to take the words of the Roman delegation seriously, they mean only that Dioscorus supported Eutyches.

But we appreciate your paper and its general trend.

FATHER ROMANIDES: In this regard the only point I wish to make in my paper is that Dioscorus supported Eutyches as one who accepts the double consubstantiality of the Only-Begotten Son of God. Only this can explain why Dioscorus' Orthodoxy was upheld at Chalcedon. On the other hand, Dioscorus was deposed for excommunicating Leo and also for acting uncanonically. I was not concerned specifically with the type of support Eutyches received from Dioscorus, although this is in itself of great importance.

BISHOP SARKISSIAN: In our new effort which aims at a deeper and more adequate understanding of the Council of Chalcedon than what we have been accustomed to in the past, we must not overlook the whole emotional, psychological climate in which the Council evolved and the political factors and tensions which were operative elements in the course of the Council. As the great majority of the bishops were Cyrillians in their theological thinking, it was strange that the Tome of Leo was taken as a standard formulation of Christology. There are several other aspects in the minutes of the Council which need to be taken into consideration in a well-balanced presentation and evaluation of the spirit and the content of the Council. In this paper, some important aspects, such as the role of Leo's Tome, the rehabilitation of Theodoret and Ibas are overlooked and only the positive elements and aspects have been taken into account. We need a fuller evaluation of the Council as a historical event.

FATHER ROMANIDES: I am surprised at some of the claims of oversight, since much of my paper is devoted to the role of Leo's Tome, the Christology of Theodoret and its relation to Leo's Christology, and the manner in which Theodoret and Ibas were rehabilitated at Chalcedon. I am also amazed that at this point in our conversations Leo's Tome is still referred to as "a standard formulation of Christology" at Chalcedon. It is easy for you to use the Latin interpretation of Chalcedon as a stick against us, but if we are to get anywhere you will have to take the Greek Chalcedonian interpretation of the place of Leo's Tome at the Fourth Council more seriously.

DR. KHELLA: In interpreting the Acts of Chalcedon it is unrealistic to expect agreement on our two sides. This paper is historically more or less accurate in what it says, but the data have been chosen from a particular perspective. As Bishop Sarkissian said, we need a more balanced study of the Acts. As for a few inaccuracies, e.g. on page 83, it is not true to say that Severus was the first to agree on two natures "in thought." Timothy Aelurus was just as correct in this regard, also Peter the Iberian and others. On pages 87-90, I feel that the role of Leo at Chalcedon should be clarified. The numbers given of bishops at Chalcedon are often legendary. Perhaps there were more than 360 bishops in fact, of whom only 7 were from the West. Two North Africans who were fleeing from the invasions were by accident at Chalcedon. There was also the Apocrisarius of Leo in Constantinople. Two others from the West spoke no Greek. These were the ones who wanted the Tome of Leo to be read.

The letter was read in a smaller committee in which only 23 bishops were present. Latin Acts have different numbers from the Greek Acts; but the Tome was not read in the second session. The session of 13th October is difficult to regard as a full session.

FATHER BOROVOY: I was afraid of this entry into the jungle of details from which there may be no easy way out. I wanted rather to count on my fingers the achievements of this day. Father Meyendorff's last two points in his paper are a definite achievement. When I heard Father Samuel saying "we are not monophysites," this was another achievement. When Bishop Sarkissian spoke of the *communicatio idiomatum* this was another achievement again. When finally I heard Professor Karmiris I felt we were very close to each other. It seems we should be able on this basis to find a uniting formula. Perhaps we are too enthusiastic and we should speak a little bit as Professor Florovsky did (as *advocatus diabolus*). I would continue in that negative line. Is there a dialogue here, or a dual monologue? We sincerely accept the defense of our non-Chalcedonian brethren for their past. Our side can also present a similar defense. If we take this line, the next step will be polemics. We say we are individual theologians. I do not consider myself as such. My Church sent me here to speak on her behalf — not for polemics, but for unity. I am here to find the common ground as suggested in Professor Karmiris' paper. All contributions on the Chalcedonian side bear an ecumenical spirit. They seek a meeting point, and even perhaps went further. The spirit of Cyril is strong. We are not against him. But we are the Church, but not the church of Cyril or Leo or Theodoret or anybody else. The Church is above them all. We need not accept everything of Cyril. His fundamental Christology is important; but no need to reject Leo and Theodoret in their positive contributions.

Historically, we should not seek to defend our own sides. History has no angels of light, nor purely dark devils. In history we find men acting, holy men, to be sure, but still men. Even in Nestorius there are many positive aspects. We must recognize both the merit and the weakness of both sides. The Holy Spirit works in the Church as a whole.

We must look for the ground of unity. The details can be worked out by a commission.

PROFESSOR ROMANIDES: There is no doubt, as Bishop Sarkissian and Professor Khella point out, that my paper is written from a certain point of view. It only happens that this point of view is that of the overwhelming majority of the Council which accepted Leo's Tome only in the light of St. Cyril's *Twelve Chapters*. That this should be the normal outcome at Chalcedon cannot be surprising when one takes seriously the historical fact that the Latins and Antiochenes, who were the only ones who unconditionally supported the Tome, were a small minority at the Council.

I am very happy to hear that Severus was not the first one on the non-Chalcedonian side who could accept *two natures tei theoriai monei after the union*. There are no indications from the minutes of the Ephesine Council of 449 that Dioscoros could accept this. Nevertheless, I should like to point out that I was not asked to write a book on Chalcedon, but only ten pages which became seventeen. The purpose of the paper did not include any discussion of such technical problems concerning the number of sessions, bishops, etc. I cannot accept the idea that Session II could have debated Leo's Tome without it having first been read. The cruciality of the debate over Leo's Tome at Session II can be seen in the fact that the bishops were given five days in which to examine St. Leo's faith in the light of St. Cyril's *Twelve Chapters*. Session IV continued the discussion and the acceptance of Leo's Tome only in the light of St. Cyril is clearly seen in the recorded opinions of the bishops and reflected in the Chalcedonian definition itself. These are incontrovertible facts and no manipulation of the minutes can mitigate their importance.

I think a very basic difficulty which we Chalcedonians of the Greek tradition face is that there is a peculiar theological alliance between the Latin (including Protestant) and non-Chalcedonian scholars in regard to Chalcedon. For the same reasons that the Westerners can accept Chalcedon, the non-Chalcedonians reject Chalcedon. Both sides try to prove that Chalcedon rejected the *Twelve Chapters* of St. Cyril and accepted Leo's Tome either as a correction (so say the Westerners) or as a distortion (so say the non-Chalcedonians) of Cyrillian Christology. Contrary to both these approaches (which do not represent the central tradition of Chalcedon) the Chalcedonian Greeks read the documents of Chalcedon in the light of Ephesus I (431) and Constantinople II (553). The usual Latin and non-Chalcedonian picture whereby our Illyrian, Thracian, Asian, Pontian, Cappadocian, Palestinian, and Egyptian Fathers are presented as capitulating before a few Latin and Antiochene bishops is caricature and not history.

In regard to the welcome remarks of Father Borovoy I would like to add that my paper is not a defense of Chalcedon, whose shortcomings I try to indicate, nor is it a defense of the non-Chalcedonian position. Rather it is an attempt to understand how the two traditions survived the complexities of history while always maintaining essentially the same Orthodox faith. Such a study so obviously calls for the tracing in history of the common central intuition of faith and doctrine which could not be distorted by the tragedies of our respective histories. This fact is living testimony to the meaning of continuity in truth which is not imposed by any external authority but which is the fruit of communion with the source of truth. To try to avoid the complexities of history when dealing with each other can lead only to a false sentimentalism which can never and will never lead to unity and can be no more effective than an ostrich burying her head in the earth to solve her immediate problems. Whether we like it or not we are christologically the Church of Cyril because Cyril's Christology is that of the Bible, the Fathers, and the Third, Fourth, Fifth and Sixth Ecumenical Councils. The anti-Cyrillian works of Theodoret on Christology were condemned by the Fifth Ecumenical Council and Leo's Tome was never accepted as a definition of faith. Cyril's *Twelve Chapters* are definitions of faith.

ONE INCARNATE NATURE OF GOD THE WORD

THE REV. PROF. V. C. SAMUEL

I. INTRODUCTION

The Person of Jesus Christ transcends so much our comprehension and linguistic expression that no formulation is adequate to describe Him. At the same time, the Church has adopted certain statements thereby setting a limit beyond which we should not go in our theological reflection with reference to His Person, although there is disagreement between the Chalcedonian and the non-Chalcedonian Churches on the question of what these statements are.[1] Even here the crucial difference between the two traditions of Churches may be said to lie in the attitude of each towards the phrase "one incarnate nature of God the Word." Thus on the whole the Western Churches are rather suspicious of this phrase. But in the East, while the Byzantine Orthodox Church is in favour of accepting it in a sort of partial way, the non-Chalcedonian Orthodox Church of the East regards it as a central linguistic tool to affirm the mystery of the Incarnation.

That the phrase came originally from Apollinarian forgeries ascribed to Athanasius of Alexandria is vigorously upheld by many modern scholars.[2] Even if this view be granted, it does not follow

---

[1] The non-Chalcedonian tradition accepts the "Nicene Creed," the Second Letter of Cyril to Nestorius, the Third Letter of Cyril to Nestorius with the Twelve Anathemas, and the Letter of Cyril to the Easterns, otherwise known as the Formulary of Reunion. It also accepts the theology of the *Henotikon* as orthodox. In the Chalcedonian tradition, many of the Western Churches are rather half-hearted in their acceptance of Cyril's Third Letter to Nestorius with the Anathemas, and no Church either in the East or in the West thinks much of the *Henotikon*. All the Chalcedonian Churches accept the *Tome of Leo* and the Chalcedonian formula of the Faith, both of which are rejected by the non-Chalcedonian body.

[2] For a summary treatment of this point, see R. V. Sellers, *Two Ancient Christologies* (London, 1954), p. 89, esp. n. 2. Panagiotes N. Trempela, «Δογματικὴ τῆς Ὀρθοδόξου Καθολικῆς Ἐκκλησίας» (Athens, 1959), vol. II,, p. 98. The present writer has not had a chance to examine the basis on which this view has been put forward by modern scholars. So his acceptance of it is only provisional.

that therefore the phrase should be discarded. For the crucial phrase in the Nicene Creed, namely "of the same substance with the Father" (ὁμοούσιον τῷ πατρί or *shewa bousia labo*), had not only a pagan origin,[3] but it had also been condemned by the Council of Antioch in 268 which excommunicated Paul of Samosata.[4] Therefore, the unorthodox origin of a term cannot be cited as an argument against its adoption by Orthodox theology, so long as the meaning assigned to it is orthodox and there is need for pressing that meaning. Cyril of Alexandria, the great bulwark of orthodoxy against the teaching of the Nestorian school in the fifth century,[5] saw in the phrase "one incarnate nature of God the Word" a most crucial linquistic tool to conserve the Church's faith in the Person of Jesus Christ.

However, like the Nicene phrase "of the same substance with the Father" which came to be misunderstood and misconstrued by various men for a long time, the phrase "one incarnate nature of God the Word" also was given different shades of erroneous meanings by men in olden times. Before taking up these heretical ideas for a brief discussion, it is necessary to look into the question of Eutyches.

II. The Teaching of Eutyches

The question as to what precisely were the ideas held by Eutyches is not easy to be answered. Two sets of statements made by him at the Home Synod of Constantinople in 448 are certainly to be considered confused, if not heretical.[6] Thus in the first place, when he was asked whether he would affirm that our Lord was "of the same substance with us" (ὁμοούσιον ἡμῖν or *Shewa bousia lan*), he answered in this way: "Since I confess my God to be the Lord of heaven and earth, I have not till this day let myself en-

---

[3] G. L. Prestige has shown in his *God in Patristic Thought* (London, 1952), p. 197, that Valentinians had used the phrase "homoousios."
[4] In defending the Council of Nicea, both Athanasius and Hilary of Poitiers acknowledge this fact and proceed to answer the problem derived from it.
[5] The fact that there are a number of modern scholars who are critical of Cyril's theology should be noted here. But to the present writer they seem to misread the theology of Cyril in their enthusiasm to defend the theology of the Antiochene school.
[6] All the statements of Eutyches referred to here are noted in Mansi, *Sacrorum conciliorum nova et amplissimo collectio*, vol. VI, 696-753, and E. Schwartz, *Acta conciliorum oecumenicorum*, II, i, pp. 122-147.

quire into His nature. That He is of the same substance with us, I have not affirmed till now, I confess." Again, "Till this day I have not said concerning the body of the Lord that it is of the same substance with us. But the Virgin is of the same substance with us, I confess." When, however, he was pressed as to how, if the mother was of the same substance with us, the Son could be otherwise, Eutyches said: "As you say now, I agree in every thing." It is clear from these statements that Eutyches was hesitant to affirm that our Lord was of the same substance with us.

Secondly, to the question of whether he would affirm that our Lord was two natures after the union, he answered: "I confess our Lord to be of two natures before the union, but after the union I confess one nature." (ὁμολογῶ ἐκ δύο φύσεων γεγενῆσθαι τὸν Κύριον ἡμῶν πρὸ τῆς ἑνώσεως, μετὰ δὲ τὴν ἕνωσιν μία φύσις ὁμολογῶ.)

Pushing these two statements to their logical conclusion, it is possible to read into Eutyches a position like this. Before God the Son became incarnate and Godhead and manhood were united in Jesus Christ, He was "of two natures."[7] When, however, the natures were united, He came to be "one nature." Since as Eutyches was reluctant to affirm that Christ was of the same substance with us, the expression "one nature" may well have meant for him that the manhood was lost, as it were, subsequent to the union.

It is this meaning that the *Tome of Leo,* some Bishops at Chalcedon, and the Chalcedonian Formula of the Faith have seen in Eutyches. The *Tome of Leo,* for instance, has made out that "using deceptive words," Eutyches said that "the Word was made Flesh in such wise as to imply that Christ having been conceived in the Virgin's womb, possessed the form of a man without a real body taken from His mother."[8] At Chalcedon Basil of Seleucia reported that for Eutyches a mere affirmation that God the Word became man by the assumption of flesh was enough to conserve the faith. (ὥστε εἰπεῖν αὐτὸν τὸν τρόπον τῆς σαρκώσεως καὶ ἐνανθρωπήσεως εἰ κατὰ πρόσληψιν σαρκὸς οἶδε τὸν Θεὸν Λόγον γενόμενον ἄνθρωπον.) The Chalcedonian Formula, referring in all probability to Eutyches, states that "others introduce a confusion and mixture,

---

[7] Unless we ascribe to Eutyches an Origenist Christology, this statement of Eutyches makes no sense. To read that into him is to make of him a thinker of eminence which he certainly was not.

[8] See T. H. Bindley, *The Oecumenical Documents of the Faith,* Methuen (London, 1950), pp. 224-231. For the Greek passage below see Mansi VI 633 B, and ACO. II, i, p. 92: 164-166.

shamelessly imagining the Nature of the flesh and of the Godhead to be one, and absurdly maintaining that the Divine Nature of the Only-begotten is by this confusion passible"; and that the Council "anathematizes those who imagine Two Natures of the Lord before the Union, but fashion anew One Nature after the Union."[9]

But there are other statements of Eutyches in which he shows that this is not his position. So in an oral statement made by him at the Home Synod of Constantinople he said: "Concerning His coming in the flesh, I confess that it happened from the flesh of the Virgin, and that He became man perfectly (τελείως) for our salvation." By this statement Eutyches did affirm a real incarnation. He made the same point still clearer in this confession of the faith. "For He Himself," affirmed Eutyches, "who is the Word of God, descended from heaven without flesh, was made flesh of the very flesh of the Virgin unchangeably and inconvertibly in a way which He Himself knew and willed. And He who is always perfect God before the ages, the Same also was made perfect man for us and for our salvation."[10] This statement was certainly not unorthodox, insufficient though we may judge it to conserve the Church's faith fully. So we have to say with J. N. D. Kelly, "The traditional picture of Eutyches, it is clear, has been formed by picking out certain of his statements and pressing them to their logical conclusion. . . . He was not a docetist or Apollinarian, nothing could have been more explicit than his affirmation of the reality and completeness of the manhood . . ."[11]

In any case, from the point of view of initiating a discussion of the issue which separates the Chalcedonian Church from the non-Chalcedonian Church, the question of whether Eutyches himself had, in fact, held the view ascribed to him by the *Tome of Leo* and the Chalcedonian Formula is not important. What is important, on the other hand, is the question as to whether the non-Chalcedonian Church has ever held the ideas thus ascribed to Eutyches. On this question the answer is quite clear. For Dioscorus of Alexandria did himself express this rejection of the ideas

---

[9] T. H. Bindley, *op. cit.*, pp. 232, 235.

[10] For the confession of Eutyches, see G. Hahn, *Bibliothek der symbole und glaubensregeln der alten kirche* (Breslau, 1897), pp. 319-320, and Mansi, *op. cit.*, v 1016 C.

[11] J. N. D. Kelly, *Early Christian Doctrines* (Adam and Charles Black, London, 1958), pp. 332-333.

read into Eutyches at Chalcedon.[12] Following him, the non-Chalcedonian Church has, throughout the centuries condemned these ideas[13] and even the person of Eutyches.

III. THE ERRONEOUS IDEAS ASSIGNED TO THE PHRASE "ONE INCARNATE NATURE OF GOD THE WORD"

Broadly speaking, these ideas may be classified under three heads. We will mention them one by one.

1. A Tendency to Ignore the Manhood of Christ

This, as we have seen, is the position ascribed to Eutyches. Whether he himself held it or not, there were men in olden times who maintained this view. Such men were called "Eutychianists." A certain John the rhetorician of Alexandria is reported to have taught "Eutychianism" during the decade after the Council of Chalcedon.[14]

According to Zacharia, John the rhetorician was a student of philosophy, who tried to combine some ideas derived from the Christian faith with his rational speculation. So he maintained that Jesus Christ was God the Word, who came into the world, being born of a virgin without conjugal relation. Being born in this way, He cannot have been fully man. So He was "one nature" in the sense that He was God, but not also man.

2. A Teaching Which Ignores Human Properties in Jesus Christ.

A more subtle position than the foregoing one, this emphasis may be illustrated by referring to Sergius the Grammarian. A correspondent of Severus of Antioch in the sixth century, Sergius expressed it in this way: "Godhead and the flesh are two *ousias*. Eternity is the property of the former and corruptibility that of the latter." In becoming man, God the Son assumed flesh which "was born supernaturally," and the flesh "did not see corruption." But "by reason of the union the human property was passed over."

---

[12] See Mansi VI 633C, and *ACO*. II, i, p. 92: 168.

[13] "Eutychianism" was opposed by the non-Chalcedonian body from the very beginning. Thus we have evidence that Theodosius of Jerusalem, who led the movement against Chalcedon in Palestine soon after the Council, and Timothy Aelurus of Alexandria condemned men who held it.

[14] See Zacharia Rhetor, *Historia Ecclesiastica*, I (Syriac), pp. 163-164.

Therefore, "it is better to say that there was one property" only in Christ.[15]

We find here an emphasis, which takes Godhead and manhood as two different *ousias*, each possessing its own property. But they were united in Christ in such a way that the human properties came to be lost in the union. Those who taught this idea took the phrase "one incarnate nature" as a convenient linguistic tool to conserve it.

It may be useful in this context to refer to the misunderstanding of the non-Chalcedonian position expressed by men of the Chalcedonian side in ancient times. John the Grammarian is referred to by Severus of Antioch to have criticized the non-Chalcedonian position as having maintained that "the Godhead and the flesh of Christ constituted one *ousia* and one nature."[16] The argument of the Grammarian may be put in this way: The non-Chalcedonian leaders were insisting that Christ was one incarnate nature, and that He was not two natures after the union. But the very emphasis that Christ was of the same substance with the Father as to Godhead and of the same substance with us as to manhood should be taken as an adequate basis for saying that He was in two natures. The non-Chalcedonian leaders were, however, opposed to the phrase "in two natures." This must be because in their view Christ was one *ousia*. In other words, the opponents of Chalcedon were considered unwilling to affirm the reality of Christ's manhood.

The answer of the non-Chalcedonian leaders to this criticism we shall see in a moment. What we should note in the present context is the fact that their position was very much misunderstood and even misinterpreted by men of the Chalcedonian side in olden times.

3. *A Teaching Which Maintains That the Manhood of Christ Was Incorruptible.*

This position was held by Julian of Halicarnassus. In fact, it

---

[15] See *Ad Nephalium*, ed. J. Lebon (Louvain, 1949), (Syriac), pp. 71-72.

[16] John the Grammarian was a critic of the non-Chalcedonian position, whose work in defense of Chalcedon was refuted by Severus in his *Liber contra impium grammaticum*. For this criticism of his, see *ibid.* ed. J. Lebon (Louvain, 1952), I (Syriac), p. 20.

had adherents in both the Chalcedonian and the non-Chalcedonian bodies in ancient times. Justinian himself adopted a form of it towards the end of his life, and Justinian was a persecutor of the non-Chalcedonian body.

The teaching of Julian may be summarized in this way.[17] God created man in the beginning essentially immortal and incorruptible. But by the sin of Adam and the consequent fall, he lost this essential property. In order to save man from this fallen state, God the Son became incarnate by uniting to Himself real and perfect manhood. But the manhood which He thus assumed was so sinless that it was the manhood of Adam before the fall, and so it was essentially impassible, immortal and incorruptible. Julian, however, maintained that Christ suffered passions and died on the cross voluntarily for us. At the same time, he insisted that the body of our Lord was from the moment of its formation in the womb of the Virgin incorruptible.

Of the many ideas which Julian emphasized, some are orthodox while others are heretical. Thus the following orthodox ideas in the teaching of Julian may be noted: (a) God the Son became incarnate by uniting to Himself real and perfect manhood. (b) As man, Christ was absolutely sinless. (c) The suffering and death which Christ endured were indispensable for our salvation, and God the Son Himself assumed them as His own.

But the following ideas of Julian seem heretical: (a) When God the Son became incarnate, He united to Himself the manhood of Adam before the fall. So it was essentially impassible and immortal. (b) The body of our Lord was incorruptible, not merely after the resurrection, but from the moment of its conception in the womb of the Virgin. (c) As man, Christ was of the same substance with us, not in the sense that His manhood was our manhood, but only in the sense that it was the essential manhood of Adam before the fall. In other words, according to Julian, the manhood was not only sinless, but it had no involvement in the fallen state of the human race.

---

[17] This discussion of Julian's teaching is based on a study of the writings of Severus of Antioch against Julian. For the early letters exchanged between them, see Zacharia, *op. cit.,* II, pp. 102-112, and for other writings, see Severi *Antiiulianistica,* A. Sanday (Beyrout, 1931) and British Museum M.S. No. 12158.

IV. THE NON-CHALCEDONIAN ORTHODOX CHURCH IN THE FACE OF THESE ERRONEOUS EMPHASES

These three positions were, in fact, not only rejected but even refuted by the leaders of the non-Chalcedonian Orthodox Church. As we have already noted, John the rhetorician lived during the decade after the Council of Chalcedon. Theodosius of Jerusalem, who led the movement against Chalcedon in Palestine soon after the Council, opposed his teaching and even wrote a treatise refuting it.[18] It is reported that he took strong measures against other "Eutychianists" in Palestine also. Timothy Aelurus, the immediate successor of Dioscorus on the See of Alexandria, was equally opposed to "Eutychianism." During his exile in Gangara Bishop Isiah of Hermopolis and Presbyter Theophilus of Alexandria left Egypt and made their home in Constantinople, where they disseminated "Eutychianist" ideas. On hearing this news, Timothy sent letters opposing them and in the end he excommunicated them.[19] Thus from the point of view of condemning "Eutychianists" and their ideas, there is no ground for doubt that the non-Chalcedonian Church has done it with as much vigour as the Chalcedonian Church. We can, in fact, say that the ancient Orthodox Church of the East which renounced the Council of Chalcedon has, from the beginning, excluded also the heresies which the Council has condemned.

The second and the third erroneous positions noted above came to be expressed during the days of Severus of Antioch. He refuted them, and, under his leadership, his section of the Church also excluded them categorically.

As we have noted, it was Sergius the Grammarian who expressed the second position. Severus answered him by saying that the affirmation of a difference of properties was the teaching of the fathers. The natures which were united in the one Christ, they affirmed, were different. "For one is uncreated, and the other is created." But while "the difference in properties of the natures" continued to be real, "the natures of which the one Christ is, are united without confusion." In this way, "the Word of life is said

---

[18] See Zacharia, *op. cit.*, pp. 161-164.

[19] For this incident and the letters which Timothy Aelurus wrote in this connection, see Zacharia, *ibid.*, pp. 185-205, and 215-216. That Timothy Aelurus opposed "Eutychianists" is mentioned even by Evagrius. See *P.G.* LXXXVI 2603 A.

to have become visible and tangible." When we think of the Emmanuel, we shall see that Godhead and manhood are different, and as we confess the union, "the difference signifying the natures of which the one Christ is" we do not ignore, "though by reason of the *hypostatic* union" we discard division.[20] In fact, it is on the ground of this admission that Severus works out his emphasis on the *communicatio idiomatum*. For he maintains that there is an exchange of properties in Christ, so that "the Word may be recognized in the properties of the flesh," and the human properties have "come to belong to the Word and the properties of the Word to the flesh."[21] A passage from the work of Severus against John the Grammarian may be quoted here to show how he maintains a recognition of the principle of difference in the one Christ.[22]

> "Those, therefore, who confess that the Lord Jesus Christ is one (made up) of Godhead and manhood, and that He is one *prosopon,* one *hypostasis,* and one nature of the Word incarnate, recognize and affirm also the difference, integrity, and otherness of the natures, of which the one Christ is ineffably formed. As they perceive this by subtle thought and contemplation of the mind, they do not take it as a ground for dividing the Emmanuel into two natures after the union."

That in maintaining this point of view Severus was not adopting a position discontinuous with the non-Chalcedonian leaders before him may be shown. As we know, the Formula of Chalcedon contains four adverbs with reference to the union of the natures in Christ, and they are ἀσυγχύτως, ἀτρέπτως, ἀδιαιρέτως and ἀχωρίστως (without confusion, change, division and separation). The Formula was adopted at Chalcedon on 22nd October 451. But on 8th October, fourteen days before this incident, Dioscorus stated at Chalcedon that in opposing the phrase "two natures after the union" or its cognate "*in* two natures," he was not speaking of confusion, division, change, or mixture (οὔτε σύγχυσιν λέγομεν, οὔτε τομήν. ἀνάθεμα τῷ λέγοντι ἢ σύγκρασιν ἢ τροπὴν ἢ ἀνάκρασιν).[23] Another equally important statement of Dioscorus made at Chalcedon should also be noted here. On one occasion he signified

---

[20] *Ad Nephalium, op. cit.,* pp. 74-77.
[21] *Ibid.,* p. 79.
[22] *Contr. Gr., op. cit.,* III, p. 106.
[23] Mansi VI 676D-677A; *ACO.* II, i, p. 112: 262-263.

that he was in agreement with the affirmation "*of* two natures after the union."²⁴ These evidences are sufficient to say that in protesting against the Council of Chalcedon, Dioscorus was not showing any sympathy for a theological position which ignored the manhood of our Lord.

All the non-Chalcedonian leaders have affirmed that in His Incarnation God the Son united to Himself manhood animated with a rational soul and of the same substance with us, that He endured in reality blameless passions of the body and the soul, and that there was no confusion or mixture of the natures in Him. Taking these emphases seriously, if we evaluate their teaching, we shall certainly see that in opposing the Council of Chalcedon they were not led by any sympathy for "Eutychianism" or monophysitism of any kind. We shall also realize that they had not interpreted the phrase "one incarnate nature of God the Word" to mean absorption of the manhood or the human property.

Severus answered also the charge of John the Grammarian that the non-Chalcedonian body was arguing, on the basis of the phrase "one incarnate nature of God the Word," that in Christ Godhead and manhood formed one *ousia*. In fact, he challenged the critic to show at least a single bit of evidence to prove his charge and made it very clear that his section of the Church did not hold that view.²⁵ This means that for Severus and the Church which he represented "one incarnate nature" did not mean "one *ousia*."

Julian of Halicarnassus was refuted by Severus. Relying on the work of R. Draguet, *Julien d'Halicarnasse et sa controverse avec Severe d'Antioche sur l'incorruptibilité du corps du Christ* (Louvain, 1924), R. V. Sellers maintains that the difference between the teaching of Severus and that of Julian is largely one of terminology.²⁶ The present writer finds it difficult to agree with this reading of the difference between Severus and Julian.²⁷ Even granting that this reading is correct, would the Chalcedonian side maintain a position more adequate than the one held by Severus?

---

²⁴ Mansi VI 692A; *ACO*. II, i, p. 120: 332.

²⁵ For this discussion of Severus, see his *Contr. Gr., op. cit.,* I, pp.20-24.

²⁶ R. V. Sellers, *The Council of Chalcedon* (S.P.C.K., 1953), pp. 309-310, note 6.

²⁷ For our reading of the difference between the two men, see above pp. 42-43.

V. Severus on "One Incarnate Nature of God the Word"

Following Cyril of Alexandria, Severus accepts four phrases with reference to the Incarnation. They are: "of (ἐκ) two natures," "*hypostatic* union," "one incarnate nature of God the Word," and "one composite nature." In his view all these phrases stand together. So in order to understand what the phrase "one incarnate nature of God the Word" means to him and to the Church which he represents the meaning of these phrases should be noted.

The crucial word in these phrases is "nature" (φύσις or *kyono*). As to its meaning, both Severus and the Chalcedonian writers of his time agree that it may be taken either in the sense of *ousia* or in that of *hypostasis*. Severus shows that *ousia* stands for him both as an equivalent of the *eidos* of Plato and as a generic term including all the members of a class. By *hypostasis* (ὑπόστασις or *qnumo*) Severus means a concrete particular in which the *ousia* (οὐσία or *ousio* [Syr.]) is individuated. In other words, for both sides "nature" means either the dynamic reality existing in the realm of ideas or the concrete object resulting from its individuation. But they disagree on the application of the word "nature" to the Person of Christ. Whereas the Grammarian takes it in the sense of *ousia*, Severus sees in it the meaning of *hypostasis*.[28]

Coming now to the phrases themselves, Severus makes it clear that Christ was "*of* (ἐκ) two natures." But by this phrase he does not sanction the expression "two natures before the union."[29] He says that "no one who has thought correctly has ever affirmed" this phrase "even in fancy."[30] For the "*Hypostasis* of God the Word existed ... before all the ages and times, He being eternally with God the Father and the Holy Spirit"; but "the flesh possessing a rational soul did not exist before the union with him."[31] The phrase "of (ἐκ) two natures" means, for Severus, two ideas. On the one hand, it conserves the emphasis that in Christ there was a union of God the Son with an individuated manhood, and on the

---

[28] Severus himself discusses the meaning of the crucial terms both in his *Contra Grammaticum* and in some of his doctrinal letters.

[29] He opposes "two natures before the union" in several places in his writings.

[30] *Contr. Gram.*, II, p. 239.

[31] *Patrologia Orientalis*, XII, pp. 190-191.

other that Christ was unceasingly a continuation of that union. So Christ was always "of (ἐκ) two natures"; and thus He was at once perfect God and perfect man being "of the same substance with God the Father" and "of the same substance with us."

The union of the natures was *hypostatic*, by which Severus means that "it was in union with the Word who is before the ages that the flesh was formed and came *to be*, and in concurrence it [namely the flesh] received with Him concreteness into the union. In this way, from two, namely Godhead and manhood, Christ is known indivisibly one Emmanuel."[32]

The phrase "*hypostatic* union," then, means for Severus that in Christ there was a coming together of everything that the Godhead of the Son implies and of everything that an individuated manhood connotes. The phrase means also the absolutely inward and personal character of the union.

In a long passage in his *Philalethes,* Severus discusses the phrase "one incarnate nature of God the Word." When the fathers spoke of "one incarnate nature of God the Word," he writes, "they made it clear that the Word did not abandon His nature"; neither did He undergo any "loss or diminution in His *hypostasis*. When they affirmed that "He became incarnate" they made it clear that "the flesh was nothing but flesh, and that it did not come into being by itself apart from the union with the Word." Again the words "became incarnate" refer to the Word's assumption of the flesh from the Virgin, an assumption by which from two natures, namely Godhead and manhood, one Christ came forth from Mary." He is at once God and man, being of the same substance with the Father as to Godhead and of the same substance with us as to manhood.[33]

There are three emphases made by the phrase "one incarnate nature." (1) It was God the Son Himself who became incarnate. (2) In becoming incarnate, He individuated manhood in union with Himself and made it His very own. (3) The incarnate Word is one Person.

The "one" in the phrase "one incarnate nature" is not a *simple one*, so that the characterization "monophysite" cannot be considered applicable to the position of Severus. As "one incarnate

---

[32] This is a passage taken from *Contr. Gram.*, II, pp. 239-241.
[33] See *Philalethes,* ed. Robert Hespel (Louvain, 1952) (Syriac), p. 139.

nature," Jesus Christ is one *composite* nature. In the Incarnation, by a divine act of condescension, God the Son willed to be so united with manhood that the two of them came together, without either of them being lost or diminished. At the same time, their union was so real and perfect that Christ was "one composite nature."

In the face of the misunderstanding expressed by the Chalcedonian tradition that the non-Chalcedonian position has ignored the manhood of Christ, we shall put together the ideas emphasized by Severus on this point.

(1) Christ's manhood was an individuated manhood, fully like and continuous with our manhood, with the single exception that it was absolutely sinless. (2) The manhood of Christ was individuated only in a *hypostatic* union with God the Son, and it continued to exist in perfection and reality in that union. Therefore, the manhood of Christ did not exist independent of its union with God the Son. (3) The union did not lead to a confusion of the manhood with, or a loss in, the Godhead; and therefore in Christ there were Godhead and manhood with their respective properties *hypostatically* united with each other. But the two should not be separated. (4) The Union brought into being one Person, and this one Person is the Person of God the Son in His incarnate state. There is a distinction between the pre-incarnate Son and the incarnate Son, so that the *Hypostasis* and *Prosopon* of Jesus Christ are not simply the *Hypostasis* and the *Prosopon* of God the Son. (5) The manhood of Christ was real, perfect, and dynamic in the union.

Having made all these emphases, why did Severus and the leaders of the non-Chalcedonian Church refuse to accept the phrase "in two natures?" In fact, both in his letters to Nephalius and in his *Liber Contra Impium Grammaticum,* Severus admits that some earlier fathers had spoken of Christ that He was two natures. These fathers, insists Severus, meant by the expression only that Christ was at once God and man. However, the Nestorian school adopted the phrase to assert a doctrine of two persons. The phrase should not, therefore, be used any longer. Severus says also that

> "When we anathematize those who affirm of the Emmanuel two natures after the union and their operations as well as properties, it is not for speaking of natures or operations or properties that we place them under condemnation;

but for saying two natures after the union and assigning the operations and properties to each of them, thereby dividing them between the natures."[34]

The passage is clear enough. Christ is "of two natures, the properties and operations of each of which are there in Him in a state of indivisible and indissoluble union. To illustrate the point, men saw Christ hunger or thirst or suffer physical and mental agony. It is right on their part to say on the ground of what they saw that Christ's manhood was the subject of these experiences. So also men saw Him heal the sick and raise the dead. It is correct again to say that the Godhead of Christ did these signs. But in Christ the hunger and all other physical disabilities were human, united with, and made His own by God the Son in His incarnate state. In the same way, the super-human words and deeds were expressions of the Godhead of the Son in union with manhood. In other words, it was the one incarnate Person who was the subject of all the words and deeds of Christ. This one incarnate Person was the "one incarnate nature of God the Word" or the "one composite nature" of the incarnate Son. When we reflect on Him, we can, in our contemplation, distinguish the two natures of Godhead and manhood and their respective properties and operations.

But the *Tome of Leo* went beyond this sound principle, and in declaring it a document of the faith the Council of Chalcedon also committed a great error. According to the *Tome,* "Each nature performs what is proper to it in communion with the other; the Word, for instance, performing what is proper to the Word, and the flesh carrying out what is proper to the flesh." A teaching of this kind does not affirm Christ's personal unity, but regards the natures as two persons. The phrase "in two natures" defined by the Council of Chalcedon must have meant the same teaching as that of Bishop Leo. So it cannot be accepted.

VI. The Real Difference Between the Chalcedonian and the Non-Chalcedonian Positions

As we have noted, the Chalcedonian East accepts the orthodoxy of the phrase "one incarnate nature of God the Word." It believes that it is even necessary to maintain this phrase as a safeguard against Nestorianism. But it adds that since the phrase can

---

[34] *Ad Nephalium*, p. 80.

be taken in a misleading sense, the expression "in two natures" should also be added to it. Thus by "in two natures" Eutychianism can be excluded, and by "one incarnate nature" Nestorianism may be kept out.

The non-Chalcedonian Church, on the other hand, maintains that these two phrases contradict each other in meaning, and that in the light of the theology of the *Tome of Leo* "in two natures" cannot have meant for the Council of Chalcedon anything more than the teaching of Nestorius. As for excluding "Eutychianism," it can be done by insisting on the phrase "of two natures" and by emphasizing that the "one incarnate nature" is "one composite nature." The real terminological difference between the two traditions can thus be seen to lie in the two prepositions of "in" (ἐν) and "of" (ἐκ).

A Word in Conclusion

It is quite clear that neither Dioscorus of Alexandria nor the non-Chalcedonian Orthodox Church took the phrase "one incarnate nature of God the Word" in order to ignore, or minimize the importance of, Christ's manhood. But they considered it crucial because it was the phrase by which they affirmed the indivisible unity of the Person of Christ. In fact, while opposing the Council of Chalcedon with reference to its positive affirmation of the faith which they believed was Nestorianism in disguise, they excluded the heresies which the Council had condemned.

Post Script

In the light of the questions raised during the discussion following the reading of this paper, the writer wishes to suggest these changes in the text with a view to bringing out the intended meaning more clearly.

1. Page 43, last three lines may be changed to: "In other words, according to Julian, the manhood of Christ was not only sinless, but was also without a real relation with the fallen human race."

2. Page 49, line 21 may be changed to: "The union resulted in the concurrence of Godhead and manhood into one Person (*hypostasis*) and this one Person . . ."

3. Page 50, lines 8-10 may be changed to: ". . . suffer physical and mental agony, and they may say on the ground of what they saw that it was Christ's manhood which underwent these experiences."

One Incarnate Nature of God the Word 91

DISCUSSION: Concerning the Paper of Father Samuel

FATHER ROMANIDES: I was very much impressed by the precision and Orthodoxy of this paper. On the basis of this exposition, I cannot see where we differ on essentials. To make myself clear, I would point out that the term *One Nature of God the Logos Incarnate* was accepted by Flavian and Eusebius, although there is strong evidence that they did not understand the exact sense in which Cyril used this phrase. We see this from Flavian's confession of faith of 449 and in the case of both Flavian and Eusebius from the minutes of Ephesus 449 and Chalcedon. The phrase was taken for granted at Chalcedon as equivalent to Cyril's other way of saying the same, *viz., One Hypostasis of God the Logos Incarnate.*

On the basis of Father Samuel's paper, I would like to ask our non-Chalcedonian brothers whether they would accept (1) the phrase *One Physis Composite* as equivalent to *One Ousia Composite,* and (2) *From Two Physeis* as equivalent to *From Two Ousiai*. For Chalcedonians both phrases are unacceptable when *physis* means *ousia* since they would then mean *one ousia in Christ after the union*. When we speak of *In Two Natures* we mean *In Two Ousiai*. Of course, the term is of Latin provenance, but as an anti-Eutychianist statement it should be considered adequate and should not be pressed for philosophical consequences according to this or that school of thought. It is accepted by us only as a statement of faith in the *double consubstantiality* of Christ and nothing more. When *physis* is synonymous with *hypostasis,* as in the theology of St. Cyril, then the terms *From Two Natures, One Nature Composite,* and *One Nature After the Union* are not only acceptable, but obviously necessary. Within the context of strict Cyrillian terminology *In Two Natures* would, of course, be impossible. Yet *In Two Ousiai* would be possible.

The teaching of Julian of Halicarnassus that the Logos united to Himself manhood as it was before the fall is not in itself wrong and is accepted by all Fathers. What is wrong with Julian's position, as pointed out by Father Samuel, is that the human nature of Christ was considered incorruptible before the resurrection. I would add that most Fathers would rather say that the human nature of Christ was by nature mortal but not by nature under the power or sentence of death and corruption which are the wages of sin. In this sense even angels are by nature mortal. Only God is by nature immortal. It is for this reason that the death of the Lord of Glory in the flesh was voluntary and not the wages of personal or inherited sin.

Two sentences in the paper seem to me to contradict the position which the paper is trying to defend. They are: (1) p. 50. "It is right on their part to say on the ground of what they saw that Christ's manhood was the subject of these experiences," an echo of Leo's Tome, and p. 49 "the union brought into being one Person," which reminds one of the Nestorian Person brought into being by the union of natures.

FATHER SAMUEL: The first sentence refers only to what men saw in Christ and thought about Him. But in Christ these experiences were experiences of God the Son incarnate. Therefore, no contradiction is implied by it.

The second sentence is based on the emphasis of Severus that there was a distinction between the pre-incarnate Son and the incarnate Son. On the strength of this emphasis Severus shows that the *hypostasis* of Jesus Christ, though it is continuous with the hypostasis of God the Son, is not simply the latter. The *hypostasis* of Jesus Christ is a composite *hypostasis* formed by the concurrence of Godhead and manhood. The second sentence aims only to make this point.

FATHER MEYENDORFF: When we refer to Christ as "One incarnate nature of God the Word" we mean that He is one *hypostasis*. We also accept the phrase "from two natures." But in these phrases the word "nature" means *ousia*.

FATHER ROMANIDES: "From two natures" is used as equivalent to "From two ousiai" by Flavian of Constantinople, but never by Cyril and the Alexandrians. The definition of the Fifth Ecumenical Council clearly accepts "From two natures" according to the Cyrillian usage also which speaks of "one nature" in Christ, but not "one ousia." Thus we of the Chalcedonian tradition are free to use the term " from two natures" in both the Flavian and Cyrillian sense, but never according to the Eutychian equation of " nature" and "ousia."

FATHER FLOROVSKY: The statement on page 49 that the manhood of Christ was absolutely sinless is not enough. We must also say that Christ was free from original sin.

CHRISTOLOGY IN THE LITURGICAL TRADITION OF THE ARMENIAN CHURCH

The Very Rev. Dr. Mesrob K. Krikorian

Sources and Authors

For the present study I have made use of all the liturgical books of the Armenian Church, i.e. the Service-book, the Ritual, the Book of the Divine Liturgy and the Hymnal. Since the Ritual of Ordination is used only on particular occasions, I have seldom quoted from it.

The present liturgy of the Church of Armenia originates from the IV-Vth centuries(in written form from the Vth). The Book of the Divine Liturgy[1] and the Ritual had virtually attained their final form in the Xth century, but the Service-book and the Hymnal were enriched with new songs, melodies and hymns until circa the XVth century. Of the later authors, it is worthy to mention the names of Yovhannes Pluz (c. 1250-1293 or 1326), Grigor of Xlath (1350-1426) and Araqel of Bitlis (XVth century).

The early and chief authors of the liturgical books are St. Grigor the Illuminator (catholicos 301-325), St. Nerses the Great (catholicos 353-373), Sahak the Parthian (348-439, catholicos 387-439), St. Mesrop Vardapet Mastoc (362-440), Yovhannes Mandakuni (catholicos 478-490) and Movses Xorenaci (Vth century). These authors[2] wrote all the essential prayers, songs and hymns of the Service-book, Hymnal and Ritual. The hymns for the feasts of Christmas and the Purification are traditionally attributed to Movses Xorenaci, the hymns of Penance to Mesrop Vardapet, those of Holy Week and of the Cross to Sahak the Parthian, whereas the hymns for the feasts of the Prophets, Apostles, Church-Fathers and of the Transfiguration of Christ were, it is said, written by Yovhannes Mandakuni. Later the most important contributions were made by Archbishop Stephanos of Siwniq (c. 688-735) who introduced the system of *canons* in the Hymnal and

---

[1] Archbishp Tiran Nersoyan, *Divine Liturgy of the Armenian Apostolic Orthodox Church* (New York, 1950), p. 295.

[2] For the authors of the Hymnal of the Armenian Church see the introduction to Hakob Anasyan's *Armenian Bibliograpry* (in Armenian), Ereven, I, 1959, pp. xliii-xlviii and lxv-lxxiv, where several printed and manuscript lists have been carefully collected.

wrote hymns *(orhnuthiwn)* for Easter; Grigor of Narek (951-1003) whose prayers, melodies and odes, mostly devoted to the Mother of God, were included in the liturgical books, and Nerses the Graceful (Nerses Clajensis, catholicos 1166-1173) who composed numerous popular hymns. The songs of Clajensis provide the theologian with plentiful christological material.

CHRIST THE SON

The christological doctrine of the Armenian Church is summarized in the "Profession of the Orthodox Faith"[3] as thus:

> "We believe in God the Logos, uncreate, begotten and originated from the Father before the eternal times; neither after nor younger, but just as the Father is Father, so with Him the Son is son."[4]

Jesus Christ is the only-begotten Son of God the Father,[5] being born through "an unspeakable birth."[6] He existed "in the bosom of the Father,"[7] before the eternities.[8] He was "in the beginning with God, and the Logos (was) God, (being) the picture of the uncreate and con-

---

[3] The "Profession of the Orthodox Faith has some similarities with the Athanasian Creed, but cannot be regarded as the "Athanasian Creed." In the Armenian Church it is confessed during ordinations and also, on festival Sundays, at the beginning of morning service. According to Yovseph Gathercean (*Hanganak hawatoy* = The Creed of the Armenian Church, Vienna, 1891, pp. 39-42) the "Profession of the Orthodox Faith" was compiled in the XIVth century by Grigor of Tathew or his School on the basis of the Nicene, Apostles' and Athanasian Creeds. Johannes Joachim Schroeder has published a Latin translation of this Creed in his *Thesaurus Linguae Armenicae* (Amsterdam, MDCCXI), and Paul Ricaut has provided an English translation of it in his book entitled *The Present State of the Greek and Armenian Churches*, anno Christi 1678 (London, 1679), pp. 411-14. The official Creed of the Armenian Church is that of Nicaea (*Divine Liturgy*, pp. 47 and 49), but I have mostly quoted from the "Profession" which is proper to the Armenians.

[4] *Zamagirq Hayastaneayc Ekelecwoy* (Service-book of the Armenian Church), Jerusalem, 1915, p. 6: "I believe in God the Son uncreated and begotten from eternity. The Father is eternal, the Son is eternal, and equal to the Father; whatsoever the Father contains, the Son contains." Cf. Ricaut, *op. cit.*, p. 412.

[5] *Divine Liturgy*, pp. 35 and 110; *Zaynqal Sarakan* (Hymnal) (Istanbul, 1838), pp. 18 and 22 (201).

[6] *Service-book*, p. 368 (probably by N. the Graceful).

[7] *Ibid.*, pp. 110, 647-48 (*Divine Liturgy*, p. 139); *Mastoc* (Ritual) (Jerusalem, 1901), p. 316.

[8] *Service-book*, pp. 385-86; *Hymnal*, 10(32), 22, 28, 29, 30, (42).

substantial with the Holy Spirit."[9] His wonderful birth from the Father can be compared with that of beam from the light:

"O Light, rising from the Light, righteous Sun, unspeakable birth of the Father, Son, thy name is praised before the sun (i.e. the rising of the sun)," etc.[10]

Christ, although born from the Father, nevertheless "was not after or junior,"[11] but equal in glory and power. He also shared the creation together with the Father and the Holy Ghost:[12]

"God the Word who is with the Father
equal in creation and power,
in the third day separated the waters,
brought forth the herbs and the plants," etc.[13]

Mankind, plunged in error and sin, needed heavenly assistance and power to be saved from moral degradation, degeneration and death. The Son fulfilled that mission and became the Saviour of mankind for all ages and generations. Being the supreme Love, he descended with love for our redemption,[14] to seek "the sheep which had strayed."[15] The doctrine of Redemption is one of the main and basic themes of the liturgical literature of the Armenian Church. In the hymns we read:

"O Word without beginning, consbustantial with the Father, who wast before all eternity, and came for the deliverance of thy creatures; we bless thee God of our fathers."[16]

Nerses the Graceful often addresses his prayers and songs to the Redeemer of the human race and beseeches him to have mercy on sinners:

"Son of God, and true God, who didst come down from the bosom of the Father; and wast incarnate of the Holy Virgin Mary for our redemption; wast crucified, and buried, and raised from the dead, and ascendedst to the Father, I have sinned against heaven, and before thee; remember me like the penitent thief,

---

[9] *Hymnal*, p. 30 (the same pp. 42, 56).
[10] *Service-book*, p. 368; cf. pp. 128, 348, and *Hymnal*, p. 29.
[11] *Service-book*, "Profession of the Orthodox Faith," p. 5.
[12] *Ibid.*, pp. 385-86.
[13] *Ibid.*, pp. 343; cf. pp. 110, 348 and 349 (all by N. Clajensis). See also *Divine Liturgy*, p. 41; *Hymnal*, p. 51.
[14] *Service-book*, p. 311 (N. Clajensis).
[15] *Hymnal*, p. 128, and *Service-book*, p. 647 (*Preces Sancti Nersetis Clajensis*, p. 138.)
[16] *Hymnal*, p. 28.

when thou comest in thy Kingdom. Have mercy on thy creatures, and on me a grievous sinner."[17]

Jesus Christ, the only begotten Son of God the Father, in order to redeem man, took upon himself the form of man and was born of the Virgin Mary:

"The Word without beginning was unoriginate as from the Father, and he took his beginning from the Virgin by being clothed with flesh. He was contained in the womb and at the same time he was with the Father, and being bounded by time he was born as God and man."[18]

The birth of Jesus was "a great and wonderful mystery,"[19] because although he came down from heaven, he did not depart from the Father:

"O unspeakable unity, thou wert born of the Virgin; but being indivisible, never didst thou depart from the bosom of the Father. We bless thee God of our fathers."[20]

The birth of Jesus was marvellous also because he did not have an earthly father, being born "without sperm":[21]

"The Child of the Father outside time, of the Virgin without sperm; the Creator of Heaven and earth today he was cherished in the arms of his mother."[22]

"O *theotokos* and holy (Mary), who bore God the Word in thy womb by conception without sperm; we glorify thee with unceasing song."[23]

The Son of God in order to save us, took on him our earthly and sinful nature through the Virgin Mary and thus killed the death-bringing sin:

"The immaterial (Son) entered (life) under law and became material, so that he might offer us, who are born of earth, to the Father. The Son of God who is in the bosom of the Father, as a forty-day old child was taken in the arms of the aged (Simeon), and proclaimed manifest as God and man."[24]

---

[17] *Preces Sancti Nersetis Clajensis*, p. 139.
[18] *Divine Liturgy*, p. 145.
[19] *Hymnal*, p. 26.
[20] *Ibid.*, p. 28; cf. p. 22.
[21] *Ibid.*, pp. 9, 13, 26 (29), 27, 32.
[22] *Ibid.*, p. 26 (29).
[23] *Ibid.*, p. 27.
[24] *Ibid.*, p. 58.

"Son of God who came from unspeakable glories to the world, and took our earthly corrupt nature; today you humanely revived our sinful forefather for eternal life. We bless thee unceasingly, together with the corps of incorporeal angels."[25]

God the Logos when taking flesh and blood, in accordance with natural laws took everything from the Virgin, except sin, and thus "the perfect God became perfect man."[26] In other words, the birth or body of Jesus was incorrupt and incorruptible:

"O Virgin Mary, in thy womb God, Christ our Saviour dwelt incorruptibly, we glorify thee."[27]

"And thou wert born from the holy Virgin with incorruptible body, we glorify thee praising unceasingly."[28]

The incorruptibility of the body of Christ, as a delicate and important problem, has been the subject of long and heated discussion and controversy. Severus of Antioch (c. 465-538) preached that "the body of the Lord was corruptible on the cross, and was subjected to corruption."[29] This false teaching of Severus was rejected and refuted by Julian of Halicarnassus (Vth-VIth century), but his followers also fell into exaggeration and went so far as to declare "the body of the Lord impassible and immortal" (i.e. even before the Resurrection).[30]

---

[25] *Ibid.*, p. 56.
[26] "Profession of the Orthodox Faith," *Service-book*, p. 6.
[27] *Hymnal*, p. 23 (48).
[28] *Ibid.*, p. 52.
[29] *Girq thltoc* (Book of Letters) (Tiflis, 1901), p. 60, Severus and his heresy have been condemned and anathematized by the Armenians, particularly by the catholicoi Nerses of Bagrewand (548-557), Yovhannes Gabetean (557-574), see *Book of letters*, pp. 56, 57 and 83, and Yovhannes Ozneci (717-728), see Erowand vardapet Ter-Minasean, *The Relations of the Armenian Church with the Syrian Churches* (in Armenian) (Ejmiacin, 1908), pp. 185-203. However, it is interesting to note that his name is not mentioned among those heretics who are anathematized during the ceremonies of ordination — see *Mec Mastoc* (Larger book of ritual) (Istanbul, 1807), pp. 259-60. The *Ritual of ordination* for clerks, deacons, priests, vardapets and supreme vardapets is to be found *ibid.*, pp. 234-343.
[30] *Xosrovik Thargmanic* (Xosrovik the Translator, VIIIth century) ed. Garegin vardapet Yovsephean (Ejmiacin, 1899), p. 163. The Julianist heresy is refuted by Xosrovik (*ibid.*, chapter V, pp. 149-83, and condemned in 726 by the Armenian-Syrian Council of Malazgirt (Manzikert), in the days of the catholicos Yovhannes Ozneci (Xosrovik, pp. 75-86, and Ter-Minasean, pp. 185-203). The name of Julian of Halicarnassus (Bodrum) is also not mentioned among the heretics anathematized during ordinations (*Ritual of ordination*, pp. 259-60).

98 *Does Chalcedon Divide or Unite?*

The Armenian Church does not accept either the theopaschite heresy of Severus, according to which Godhead in Christ suffered on the cross, or the opinion of the Julianist Phantasiastae, who taught a sort of phenomenalism and believed that the body of Jesus Christ was uncorrupt and incorruptible, and that Christ, as the unspeakable real unity of perfect God and perfect man, suffered on the cross:

"The Armenian Church's doctrine is similar to that of Julian, in not saying that the body of Christ was subjected to corruption necessarily and from the beginning, which would be to dishonour the unity (of the body) with Godhead, but she does not thus become Julianist and phenomenalist. Moreover adding the word 'who wast crucified' in the Trisagion for the person of Christ in view of the unspeakable unity, does not imply that she approves of theopaschism."[31]

The following hymn presents the doctrine of the Armenian Church in connection with the theopaschite and phenomenalist controversies:

"(O Christ) who art of uncreate Godhead and unchangeable nature, who wast born of the Virgin in the form of the first-created, and came willingly to sufferings; we beseech thee have mercy on thy creatures."[32]

The Redemption of man was a process which the Son of God fulfilled. It started with the wonderful Incarnation of Christ, was expressed by his preaching and miracles; effected through the Passion on the cross; continued by his death, and was concluded with his triumphant Resurrection. Christ suffered for us in order to save us from sin and from the condemnation for sin:

"With our nature which thou didst put on
wast crucified on the cross,
releasing us from sins,
from the bonds of our forefather."[33]

Christ underwent the Passion for our salvation humbly[34] and willingly and in the harmonious unity of God and man:

"(Christ) was sadly concerned about the Passion
in Three being lonely;

---

[31] M. Ormanean, *Azgapatum* (History of the Armenian Nation), vol. I (Istanbul, 1912), p. 841.
[32] *Hymnal*, p. 279.
[33] *Service-book*, pp. 115-16 (by N. the Graceful).
[34] *Ibid.*, p. 112 (N. the Graceful).

'My soul is willing to save the world,
but the nature of my body is weak.'
Not the one (nature) was strong and powerful,
and the other feeble and unsafe,
but being one and the same unity,
bore the sufferings willingly."[35]

The death of Jesus Christ is the triumph over death for all men who believed and would believe in him:

"Only begotten Son and Word of God and immortal being (=essence), who didst deign to become incarnate through the holy and ever-virgin Mother of God;

"Thou, unchangeable as thou art, didst become man and wast crucified and didst trample down death by death."[36]

By his miraculous Resurrection Christ granted us new and eternal life:

"Christ is risen from the dead! He trampled down death by death, and by his Resurrection he granted life unto us, glory unto him for all ages. Amen."[37]

Rising from the dead, Christ shined forth as a light[38] and promised us eternal life:

"The incorporeal angels gathering
near the life-giving and holy Sepulchre,
give the message of eternal life to the human race."[39]

After his Resurrection he ascended into heaven and sent us the Holy Spirit of consolation and grace:

"And arising unto heaven and
ascending on the wings of the winds,
he rose in the *same* body
with which he died and rose again.
And as a good tiding,
thou didst promise to grant to them the Spirit of the Father,
and thereafter blessing them, Lord,
thou didst ascend into heaven with glory,
and our human nature,

---

[35] *Ibid.*, pp. 71-72 (N. the Graceful).
[36] *Divine Liturgy*, introit (The Monogenes), p. 35 (and 131).
[37] *Ibid.*, introit for Easter day, p. 157 (*Service-book*, p. 426).
[38] *Service-book*, p. 117 (*Divine Liturgy*, p. 113).
[39] *Ibid.*, p. 117.

which the Evil one made fit for hades,
thou didst lift higher
than the nature of the fiery spirits."[40]

Christ will come again with the same body and with the glory of the Father to judge the quick and the dead, "and that (will be) the resurrection of all men."[41] Still in the "Profession of the Orthodox Faith" we read:

"We believe also in reward for deeds; eternal life for the righteous and everlasting suffering for sinners."[42]

Nerses Clajensis in the following songs gives a vivid picture of the last judgment by the Son at the end of the world:

"Thou sittest on the Lord's throne,
receiving adoration from the creatures.
Thou judgest the world righteously,
recompensing reward according to deeds," etc.[43]

"Secrets of men are exposed,
every single one which is committed;
deeds of good will be crowned,
those of evil will be thrown in the unquenchable fire."[44]

QUESTION OF CHRIST'S NATURES

The Son of God, the Logos who was from the beginning, at the right time came into the world to save men from evil, sin and death. From the Virgin Mary "he took body, soul and mind and everything that is (in) man,"[45] except sin,[46] and perfect God became perfect man, truly and not by supposition.[47] In the "Profession of the Orthodox Faith" the Incarnation of Jesus Christ is formulated as the following:

---

[40] *Divine Liturgy*, p. 159.

[41] "Profession of the Orthodox Faith," *Service-book*, p. 7 (the Nicene Creed, *Divine Liturgy*, p. 49) and Ricaut, p. 414.

[42] *Service-book, ibid.*, and Ricaut, *ibid.*

[43] *Ibid.*, p. 119.

[44] *Ibid.*, pp. 9-20.

[45] Nicene Creed, *Divine Liturgy*, p. 47.

[46] The usual Nicene Creed of the Armenian Church does not contain the expression "except sin" (χωρὶς ἁμαρτίας), but it does exist in the text of Nerses of Lampron (XIIth century), see his *Xorhrdacuthiwm srbazan pataragi* (Commentary of divine liturgy) (Jerusalem, 1842), p. 56.

[47] In the Armenian text of the Nicene Creed it is said "truly and not by supposition," but (Archbishop) Tiran Nersoyan (*Divine Liturgy*, p. 47) has translated it as "truly and not in semblance." (!)

Christology in Armenian Liturgical Tradition 101

"We believe that one of the three Persons, God the Word was born from the Father before all eternity; in time descending into the virgin Mary, and taking her blood he united it with his Godhead. Nine months he patiently remained in the womb of the spotless Virgin, and the perfect God became perfect man, with soul, mind and body; one person, one countenance, and one united nature. God became man without any change or transformation; conceived without sperm and having an incorruptible birth. As his Godhead has no beginning, likewise there is no end for his humanity, for as Jesus Christ was yesterday and (is) today, so he will be the same for ever."[48]

Since the IVth century the Incarnation of Jesus Christ has been a subject of controversial discussion. Until the Vth century, the Armenian Church faced and refuted the false teachings of the heretics within the framework of the ecumenical Church, and thereafter with the Oriental Orthodox Churches. In the IVth century Arius of Alexandria denied the consubstantiality of Christ. In 325 three hundred and eighteen church-fathers assembled at Nicaea and, condemning the Arian heresy, re-established the preaching of the Apostles as the foundation-stone of faith for the holy Church:[49]

"Today the holy fathers preached the Word as being from the beginning, and as having been born unspeakably from the Father before the eternity; being with the Father creator from eternity and consubstantial with the Spirit."[50]

"I saw in that council word emanating from the Father and confessing (Christ) as born and yet his not being a creature, being always consubstantial with the Father and the Holy Ghost. And (the fathers) refuted the heresy with luminous words and anathematized Arius and his blasphemous sect."[51]

In the 5th century Nestorius patriarch of Constantinople (428-431) claimed that Christ had distinct divine and human persons. He thought and taught that "Mary did not bear God, but the creature man, as one of the prophets, yet he (Christ) was greater than the prophets, because he became the temple of God the Word."[52]

In 431 the ecumenical Church assembled at Ephesus, condemned

---

[48] *Service-book,* p. 6; cf. Ricaut, pp. 412-13.
[49] *Hymnal,* p. 433; *Book of letters,* pp. 44-45.
[50] *Hymnal,* p. 433.
[51] *Ibid.,* p. 437; see also *Ritual of ordination,* p. 259.
[52] *Book of letters,* p. 67.

the heresy of Nestorius, proclaimed the Virgin Mary as *theotokos* (=Mother of God), stated that Christ, born of Mary was not only man, but God and man at the same time, and affirmed the formula of Cyril of Alexandria, "one is the nature of the incarnate Word" (or "the incarnated Word had one nature"):

> "The Word was clothed in the body and the incorporeal became incarnate with a united nature from the two; he suffered on the four-winged cross and rose again from the dead uncorrupt. (The fathers) anathematized Nestorius and his blasphemous sect."[53]

In the divine liturgy of the Armenian Church the Incarnation of Christ is explained with admirable clarity in the following terms:

> "For having become man truly and without phantasm and having become incarnate, in unity without confusion, from the Mother of God and holy virgin Mary, he underwent all the passions of our human life without sin," etc.[54]

In very many hymns it is emphasized that the one born of the Virgin Mary was God and man,[55] and that Mary was *theotokos*. Here I quote a stanza:

> "The Son who was before all eternity, today appeared in the world as God and perfect man," etc.[56]

The title *theotokos* is commonly used for the Mother of God in the hymns:

> "The holy Church confesses as incorrupt and *theotokos* the virgin Mary through whom the bread of immortality and the cup of rejoicing were given to us," etc.[57]

In the Vth century Eutyches of Alexandria, who was a zealous Cyrillian, went so far in his struggle against Nestorian heresy as to doubt the full human nature of Christ. He is supposed to have believed that the Son of God appeared in the world in the semblance of man, but that he was not consubstantial with us.[58] At the council of Chalcedon

---

[53] *Hymnal*, p. 437; cf. *Ritual of ordination*, p. 259, the bishop asks the candidate: "Do you renounce and anathematize Nestorius who confesses Christ as man and does not acknowledge the holy virgin Mary as *theotokos*, and (asserts) the one born from her altogether not God, but only man?" And the candidate replies: "I renounce and anathematize."

[54] *Divine Liturgy*, p. 67.

[55] Ibid., p. 30.

[56] *Ibid.*, p. 30 (42).

[57] *Ibid.*, p. 33.

[58] *Book of letters*, p. 66. Eutyches, as well as the Council of Chalcedon,

Christology in Armenian Liturgical Tradition 103

in 451 Eutyches was condemned, the Tome of Pope Leo I was ratified, and the doctrine of the existence of two natures, two wills and two actions in Christ was proclaimed. The Orthodox churches of Egypt, Syria and Armenia[59] rejected the Chalcedonian doctrine. Long-lasting controversies took place involving Byzantine Emperors in the struggle, but the doctrine was re-affirmed at the fifth (553) and sixth (680) "Ecumenical Councils," as well as by the Councils of the Lateran (649) and of Toledo (675), and finally "Chalcedon triumphed, but over ruins."[60] According to Chalcedonian doctrine, the divine and human natures in Christ were united through the hypostasis of God the Word. In other words, the Son of God uniting human nature with his divine personality possessed two natures, divine and human, with two wills and two actions. Contrary to the dogma of *two natures,* the Coptic, Syrian and Armenian Churches proclaim one wonderful and unspeakable *unity of two natures* in Christ, and confess the one born of the Virgin Mary as real man and at the same time God, and with divinity adore humanity, and with humanity adore divinity.[61] In hymns of the Armenian Church the formula of "the unspeakable unity" of Christ[62] is repeatedly declared and the fact that through the unspeakable unity Christ was perfect man at the same time perfect God, is clearly emphasized.[63] Of course, one must not expect to find detailed

---

were condemned by the Armenian Church in 508 at the second session of the Council of Dowin, during the reign of catholicos Babgen I from Othmus (*Book of letters,* pp. 48-51; M. Ormanean, *History of the Armenian Nation,* I, pp. 509-511). In the *Ritual of ordination* (p. 260) we read: The bishop asks: "Do you anathematize Eutyches who denied justification by grace of Christ?" The candidate replies: "I renounce and anathematize."

[59] In 451 the Armenians were fighting against the Persians and Mazdaism and were defending Christianity with their blood and so did not take part in the Council of Chalcedon. In 508, at the second session of the Council of Dowin, the doctrine of Chalcedon was officially condemned as a sort of Nestorianism and diophysism (*Book of letters,* pp. 48-51, and Ormanean's *History of the Armenian Nation,* I, pp. 509-511).

[60] Henri Grégoire, "The Byzantine Church" in *Byzantium,* ed. N. H. Baynes and H. St. L. B. Moss (Oxford, 1961), p. 104: "Chalcedon triumphed, but over ruins: it triumphed despite the power and the genius of Zeno, of Anastasius, of Justinian, of Theodora, and of Heraclius who for more than two centuries had sought with admirable devotion and perfect clear-sightedness to disarm hatreds, to conciliate the rival mysticism. They had matched themselves against forces which were too strong for them."

[61] *Book of letters,* pp. 48-49.

[62] *Hymnal,* p. 28, etc.

[63] *Ibid.,* pp. 29, 30, 36, 38, 51, 52, etc.

christological explanations in hymns, nevertheless they provide us with a reflection of the Orthodox doctrine of the Church in definite and explicit words and assertions. I give some examples:

> "We beseech thee O Son of the eternal Father, who wast born today from the Virgin, being in nature the first created, God and man, have mercy upon us."[64]

> "The Creator of heaven and earth, being God and Man, appeared in the stream of the river Jordan, his body united with the divinity, and washed the world from sins; glorify him for ever."[65]

> "The Word without beginning originating from the Virgin appeared in flesh in the world, and was seen by the heralds of the true Word and proclaimed to the universe as God and man."[66]

For many centuries a hymn of three verses condemning the Council of Chalcedon and the Tome of Leo was used in the Armenian Church on the feast-day of the Fathers of the Church, but at the beginning of XVIIIth century (1726-1727) it was dropped during efforts to reconcile the Armenian Catholic community with the mother Church. Here I quote only the last stanza:

> "Beautiful shoot, springing afresh from the roots of the holy fathers, flower of faith, great witness of Christ, holy Dioscorus, in disagreement with the unlawful Council, anathematized Leo and his blasphemous Tome."[67]

CONCLUSION

The Armenian Church has shown a sign of tolerance even before the Ecumenical movement omitting the hymn which condemned the Council of Chalcedon and the Tome of Leo. I hope in agreement with sister Churches she will drop also the anathemas from the Ritual of ordination thus suppressing the sad traces of the past and opening the way for mutual tolerance, love and co-operation.

---

[64] *Ibid.*, p. 38.
[65] *Ibid.*, p. 51.
[66] *Ibid.*, p. 70 (78, 87).
[67] *Manuscript Hymnal* of Antelias (Lebanon), by the scribe Karapet Cicol, dating from 1320, pp. 552-53. In the *Ritual of ordination* (p. 260), we read: The Bishop asks: "Do you anathematize Leo the heretic and his blasphemous Tome which he wrote dividing in two the one?" (Jesus Christ). And the candidate replies: "I renounce and anathematize."

Christology in Armenian Liturgical Tradition

DISCUSSION: Concerning the paper of Dr. Mesrob Krikorian

6. Comments on the paper of Father Krikorian:

ROMANIDES: The humanity of Christ before the resurrection is mortal (θνητή). The death of Christ is the corruption (φθορά) of His human nature which is a separation of the soul from the body, but not a separation of the soul or body from the hypostatic union with the Logos. This corruption (φθορά) or death of the humanity of Christ, however, is not a dissolution or decomposition (διαφθορά) of soul or body. Christ never became a corpse with members decomposing as heretically depicted in some Protestant and Roman Catholic paintings.

I would like to ask if these distinctions are to be found in the theology of Severus. The heresy of Julian was that the body of Christ before the resurrection was incorruptible (ἄφθαρτος).

V. C. SAMUEL: According to Severus of Antioch, Christ's body was mortal and corruptible before the resurrection. The word "corruptibility" meant for him the ability to suffer and die in a real sense. Attention should be drawn to the fact that the quotation in the last paragraph on page 8 of Father Krikorian's paper is contradicted on page 9. It is questionable whether the Armenian tradition which rejects Severus has really understood him. In his ecclesiastical history Michael the Syrian notes that in 726 A.D. the Syrian and the Armenian Churches reached an agreement on the question at issue. This incident should be respected.

KRIKORIAN: In recent times the teachings of Severus and of Julian have been closely examined by the Armenian Church especially by the patriarch Malachia Ormanian, Archbishop Garegin Yorsephian and Professor Erowand Ter-Minassian.

DAMASCINOS: I did not say that the texts were translated from the Syriac or the Greek. I only said that the translations spread by the Syrian monophysites were given Nestorian nuances. There are Armenian writers that reproach Chalcedonians as follows: Sometimes they call one and the same Christ as unique and one-personal, the Son of God and the only-begotten Lord, and again they teach him to be unmingled of two natures; and they say that those who think Christ's two natures — his whole manhood and his whole godhead — to be mingled, are to be anathematized. Now if there are two natures unmixed and unchangeable, one believes in a fourfold Trinity. From this belief the Nestorianizing tendencies of the Fourth Ecumenical Council were condemned. Concerning the incorruptibility of the body of Christ we find the influence of Julian in other Armenian writers: "Those who dare call Him corruptible are anathematized by the holy Fathers who say: He who dares call the life-giving death of the Lord and His redeeming passion corruptible as if it were that of a simple man, and does not confess that in His passion He was impassible and in His death immortal as being God to whom all things are possible, let him be anathematized."

KRIKORIAN: Chalcedon is rejected by the Armenian Church not because of its content but also for definite historical reasons.

BISHOP SAMUEL: Ten years ago a consultation of theologians from the Greek Patriarchate of Alexandria worked on much the same theme as that of Krikorian and no theological differences had been found to exist between the Chalcedonian and non-Chalcedonian Churches. It is known that terminology differs between the two traditions of churches but there is the same underlying theology although it is worked out differently in practice. There has existed in Alexandria a joint committee with representatives on it of the Greek Orthodox, Armenian and Coptic Churches. The group is an unofficial one and its findings are not published.

THE ORTHODOX FAITH IN THE LITURGIES AND PRAYERS OF THE COPTIC CHURCH

Dr. Hakim Amin

The scope of the present paper is to set forth the Orthodox Faith as it is proclaimed in the Liturgies and Prayers of the Coptic Church.

The Orthodox Faith

The Orthodox Faith according to our profession is that our Lord is perfect in His Godhead, and perfect in His Manhood. However, we dare not say that He is God and Man together, for this expression implies separation. He is rather God Incarnate. The Godhead and the Manhood are united in Him in a complete union, i.e. in essence, hypostasis and nature. There is no separation or division between the Godhead and the Manhood in our Lord. From the very moment of the descent of the Divine Word, in the Virgin's Womb, the Second Person of the Blessed Trinity took to Himself from St. Mary's Blood a human body with a human rational soul, and made Himself One with the Manhood which He received from the Holy Virgin. The One born of St. Mary, therefore, is God Incarnate, One Essence, One Person, One Hypostasis, One Nature. Or we may say that He is One Nature out of two natures. In other words, we may speak of two natures before the union took place, but after the union there is but One Nature, One Nature having the properties of the two natures.[1]

While the Coptic Church repeats this belief in diffcrent parts of her anaphorae, it is clear that the creed is added as the important element in most of the Church Prayers — especially the anaphorae — to enable the faithful to understand their Orthodox Faith.

The Coptic Church uses three anaphorae; that of St. Basil which is the one in general use throughout the year, that of St. Gregory which is used for the feasts, especially the feasts of the Nativity of Jesus Christ, the Epiphany and Easter; and that of St. Cyril, otherwise known as that of St. Mark, which, though displaying definite Egyptian characteristics, is seldom used at the present day.

---

[1] Bishop Gregorius, *The Christological Teaching of the Non-Chalcedonian Churches*, p. 6.

In the following extracts from the Coptic Church Prayers, we realize the explicit soundness of the belief of the Coptic Church.

I. IN THE PRAYERS OF RAISING OF INCENSE:

1. In many of the prayers, especially in the Prayer of Thanksgiving, there is mention of the expression: "The Only Begotten Son, Our Lord and God." The Prayer of Thanksgiving, for instance, ends with: "With goodness, mercy, and the love of mankind which are for the Only Begotten Son, our Lord, our God and Saviour Jesus Christ."[2]

2. In the early morning Prayer (raising of incense) or evening Prayer, the priest raises three times the incense burner, addressing the Holy Virgin. In the first raising of incense he says:

"Rejoice, O Mary, the beautiful dove, that begat for us God the Word, we greet thee."

In the second raising he says:

"Hail to thee, Virgin, the real and true Queen; greetings to the pride of our race. She begat for us Emmanuel."

In the third raising he says:

"We ask thee, our honest intercessor, to remember us before our Lord Jesus Christ in order that He may forgive us our sins."[3]

In the raising of the incense of the morning, the priest says inaudibly after a reading from the Acts:

"Jesus Christ is He Himself in the past, today and forever. In one hypostasis we bow to Him and glorify Him."

3. At the end of the Prayer for the raising of incense, the priest mentions the name of the Angel, Apostle, Martyr or Saint to whom the occasion is dedicated. He says:

"The Blessings of the Mother of God, the Pure Saint, Mary."[4]

4. The priest then dismisses the people, telling them:

"The peace and love of Jesus our Christ be with you all, go in peace."[5]

This the "Kholagi" gives in Greek:

«Ἡ εἰρήνη καὶ ἀγάπη τοῦ Ἰησοῦ Χριστοῦ ἡμῶν μετὰ πάντων. Πορεύεσθε ἐν εἰρήνῃ».

---

[2] "Kholagi Al- Mokaddas" (The Book of the Holy Mass), p. 29; see also 2 Peter 1:11.
[3] *Ibid.*, pp. 47, 48; see also Matt. 1:18-25 and John 1:1-14.
[4] *Ibid.*, p. 145.
[5] *Ibid.*, p. 148; see also Acts 16:36.

At Christmas and Epiphany, the following blessing is given for dismissal:

"My Lord, Jesus Christ, Begotten of the Father, before all ages, who took flesh from the Virgin Mary and was born on earth in Bethlehem of Judea, who saved us from our sins. He who gives light to everyone brought into the world, illumine our hearts, and grant us the blessing of Thy Virgin birth . . ."[6]

II. IN ST. BASIL'S ANAPHORA:

1. The following hymn is chanted at the time the priest goes to the people before the raising of the incense to St. Paul:

"The golden incense-burner is the Virgin, and its scent is our Saviour. She begat Him, and He saved us and forgave us our sins."[7]

2. At the end of the reading of the "Catholicon" in Arabic, the people chant the following:

"God wipes away the sins of the people through their sacrifices and the burning of incense. He who gave up Himself on the cross as an accepted ransom to redeem our race."[8]

We have to notice that each anaphora is preceded by a mass for the Catechumens, a part of which is the reading of the Coptic Synaxarion. The occasional biographies of the Martyrs of the day are read including sometimes portions from the sayings of certain saints about the Faith. The Orthodox Faith is expressed in the Coptic Synaxarion as follows:

The union of the Word of God with the Flesh is as the union of the Soul with the Body, and as the union of fire with iron, which although they are of different natures, yet by their union they become one. Likewise, the Lord Christ is one Christ, one Lord, one Nature, and one Will.[9]

So also, at the crucifixion of Jesus Christ, though the Divine and Human natures were indissolubly united in the One Person of Jesus Christ on the cross, yet it was the Human Nature above that suffered, and in no wise the Divine Nature.

---

[6] The Book of the Holy Mass, p. 160; see also Psalms 2:7.
[7] The Book of the Holy Mass, p. 233; see also John 1:1-3 and John 1:14 and Matt. 1:18-25.
[8] *Ibid.*, p. 248.
[9] R. Basset: "Le Synaxaire Arabe Jacobite in Patrologia Orientalis," t. 1, fasc. 3, p. 23.

3. Before each of the anaphorae, the faithful repeat the creed: the creed which is the same as that of the Greek Church with the following slight differences:
   a) The first person plural is used wherever the Greek text has the first person singular (We believe, instead of I believe);
   b) "All things visible" — the Coptic omits "all";
   c) The Coptic has "We believe in One Lord Jesus Christ";
   d) After the words "He rose," the Coptic adds "from the dead";
   e) For "at the right hand of the Father," the Coptic has "His Father";
   f) And for "And in the Holy Spirit," the Coptic has "Yea, we believe in the Holy Spirit."[10]

4. In the Prayer of reconciliation, the priest says:

"O Great and Eternal God, He who made man without corruption, and through the life-giving appearance of Thy Only Son, our Lord and God, our Saviour Jesus Christ, Thou hast destroyed death that entered the world through Satan's envy."[11]

5. After the Prayer of reconciliation, the people chant the following hymn "Isbismos":

"Rejoice, O Mary, the slave and the Mother, for He who lies on thy lap is praised by the angels, and the cherubim and seraphim bow down to Him and sing His praises. We have no favour with our Lord Jesus Christ save through thy requests and intercessions, O Mother of God, our Lady."[12]

There is another hymn "Isbismos" which could be chanted in place of the above:

". . . Blessed art Thou who art our hope. Blessed art Thou, O Son of God. Blessed art Thou Jesus Christ, and Thy Mother the Virgin St. Mary, the beautiful dove. Mary, the Mother of God (Theotokos). Mary, the Mother of Jesus Christ. To Thee be glory and honour . . ."[13]

6. In the Prayer of blessings that comes after that, the priest says:

"Blessed, blessed, blessed. O True God, our Lord, He who created us, sustained us, and put us in Paradise. And once we

---

[10] O. H. E. Khs-Burmester: "The Rites and Ceremonies of the Coptic Church," in E.C.Q., Vol. VII, No. 6 (April-June, 1948), p. 399.
[11] *Ibid.*
[12] The Book of the Holy Mass, p. 304.
[13] *Ibid.*, pp. 312-315.

were tricked by the serpent and broke Thy commandment, we fell from eternal life, and were sent out of Paradise. Yet Thou didst not leave us to perish, but always sent us Thy Prophets, and at the end of the days through Thy only Begotten Son, our Lord God, our Saviour Jesus Christ, Thou appeared to us; we who were in darkness and in the shadow of death. For He who was conceived of the Holy Spirit and the Virgin Mary, became man and taught us the way of salvation."[14]

7. In the Prayer before Confession, the priest holds the "Spediakon,"* and after he dips it in the chalice, does the sign of the cross with it on the Holy Body in the plate, and returns it to the chalice saying:

"Blessings to the Holy ones, Blessed be our Lord Jesus Christ, Son of God, and the Holy Spirit. Amen."

The people answer:

"Amen. One is the Blessed Father, One is the Blessed Son, One is the Holy Spirit. Amen."

Then he divides the Body and puts three sections in his left hand, repeating the first part of the Confession:

"The truly blessed and sanctified Body and Blood of Jesus Christ, Son of our God. Amen."[15]

After repeating this three times and the people answer "Amen," the priest goes on with the rest of the Confession:

"Amen, amen, amen. I believe, I believe. I believe and confess to the last breath that this is the life-giving Flesh, that of the Only-Begotten Son, our Lord and our God, our Saviour Jesus Christ. He took it from our Lady and Queen, the Mother of God, the Pure and Holy St. Mary, and made it one with His Divinity without mingling and without confusion and without alteration. He confessed the good confession before Pontius Pilate, and by His own will He gave Himself up on the cross to redeem us. In truth, I believe that His Divinity was never separated from His Humanity for one moment nor for a wink of the eye. This is given for our redemption, forgiveness, and eternal life for those who partake from it. I believe, I believe, I believe that this is the truth. Amen." [16]

---

[14] *Ibid.,* pp. 319, 320; see also Genesis 3:7-17.
* The Spediakon is the middle part of the sacred Bread.
[15] The Book of the Holy Mass, pp. 398, 399.
[16] The Book of the Holy Mass, pp. 400-402.

III. In the Gregorian Anaphora:

1. This mass starts with the Prayer of the veil which the priest repeats inaudibly:

> "And also we return to Thee, O God of goodness, by coming closer to Thy Holy Altar. We beseech Thee, Thou Word, cleanse us at this time, Thou who comest with an unchangeable Body and fillest us all with Thy limitless Divinity."[17]

Then the priest repeats the following Prayer of reconciliation to the Son:

> "Thou Eternal, who existeth forever. Thou the homoousion, Creator, seated beside Himself, and Partner with the Father. He who for goodness and out of nothing created man and put him in Paradise, and when he fell through the temptation of the enemy, and disobedience of Thy Holy commandment, Thou wert willing to renew him and to return him to his first position. To save us, Thou didst not trust an Angel, or Archangel, or Prophet; but lowered Thyself unto us and took the shape of man to be like us except in sin; and became our mediator with the Father. Thus breaking the wall of partition, and destroying the old enmity, Thou hast bound those of the earth with those in heaven, and made the two one, and when Thy Body arose unto heaven, Thou didst fill us all with Thy Divinity . . ."[18]

2. And the priest says the following introduction before the "Fraction":

> "Our Lord and Saviour, Lover of mankind, the Good and Life-giving, O God who gave up Himself to redeem us from our sins, He who because of His manifold mercy dissolved the enmity of man, O Thou our Only God who is in the Bosom of the Father — Bless us, O God."[19]

3. The priest divides the Holy Body repeating the Prayer of "Fraction" to the Son:

> "Blessed art Thou, O Christ our God, the Almighty and Saviour of Thy people, O Wise Word of God, and Visible Man, Thou who because of Thy inconceivable incarnation hast prepared for us a heavenly bread, Thy Holy Body, Mysterious and Blessed in every way. Thou hast mixed for us a cup from a true vine

---

[17] *Ibid.*, p. 445.
[18] *Ibid.*, pp. 449-450.
[19] *Ibid.*, pp. 517-518.

which is Thy unpolluted Holy Side. This is that which oozed with water and blood after Thou hadst given out the Holy Spirit . . ."[20]

IV. IN ST. MARK'S ANAPHORA COMPILED BY ST. CYRIL THE GREAT:

1. After thrice doing the sign of the cross on the Bread and the Wine, the priest points to them with his finger and says:

". . . for Thy only Son, our Lord and God, our Saviour and King Jesus Christ. In the evening when He surrenderd Himself to pain and death to suffer for our sins, which He alone by His will . . . accepted unto Himself . . ."[21]

2. In another piece, the priest prays saying:

"And now, O God, Father Almighty, as we preach the death of Thy only Son, our Lord and God, our Saviour and King, Jesus Christ, and confess His resurrection, His ascension, and sitting on Thy right hand, O Father, we wait at the end of this world for His second appearance at the end of all ages full of awe and glory."[22]

V. THE PRAYERS OF "FRACTION"

1. For a Prayer of "Fraction" for the Father repeated before and during Christmas, the priest says:

"Our Father and our Master, our God the Creator, the Invisible, the Uninvolved, the Non-alterable, the Incomprehensible, He who sent His true and only light Jesus Christ, the Word, existing in the Bosom of His Father at all times, He who came to the Pure Virgin's Womb, She bore Him in complete virginity, while the angels praise Him, and the inhabitants of the heavens sing for Him crying: "Glory, glory, glory to the Lord of Saboath."[23]

2. Here is a Prayer of "Fraction" for the Son, said at Easter:

"O Christ our God, High Priest of goodness, King of all ages, Immortal, Eternal, Word of God who bestowed upon us this great sacrament which is His Holy Body and Sacred Blood for the forgiveness of our sins. This is the Flesh which He took from our Lady and Queen St. Mary, and made it one with His Divinity.

---

[20] The Book of the Holy Mass, pp. 520-521.
[21] *Ibid.*, p. 637.
[22] *Ibid.*, p. 632.
[23] *Ibid., pp.* 668-669.

This is He who descended unto hell and removed the sting of death. This is He who conquered and favoured His people. He lifted up His Saints with Him, offering them as living sacrifices to His Father. By tasting death on our behalf, He saved the living and gave mercy to the departed. And we also that sat in darkness, He bestowed upon us the light of His resurrection, through His pure Incarnation . . ."[24]

3. Here is a Syrian Prayer of "Fraction" translated from the Syrian mass into Arabic, and from Arabic into Coptic:

"This is in truth how the Word of God suffered in Flesh, and was killed and bent over the cross, and His Soul separated from His Body. Yet, His Divinity never separated either from His Soul or from His Body. His side was stabbed with a spear, when water and blood oozed out and smeared His Body for the forgiveness of the whole world. Then His Soul united with His Body. As the world was living in sin, the Son died on the cross to save us and turn us from left to right. With the Blood of His cross, He brought security to the world and united the heavenly with peoples on earth, and united the Soul with the Body. And on the third day He arose from the grave. One is Emmanuel, Wise Parable after union, and undivided into two natures. This is how we believe and how we confess. We acknowledge that this Flesh belongs to this Blood, and this Blood belongs to this Flesh. Thou art our Messiah, our God. He who for our sake was stabbed on the side in Golgotha in Jerusalem. Thou art the Lamb of God, bearer of the sins of the world. Forgive us our sins. Retain us on Thy right side . . ."[25]

VI. IN THE THEOTOKIA:

The Theotokia are arranged for week-days and are recited every day. Yassa Abdel-Messih found in the Library of the Monastery of St. Catherine on Mount Sinai among the Arabic manuscripts the two manuscripts Nos. 227 and 273 which contain the text of these seven Theotokia. He says that it seems that these Theotokia are not translated from Greek or from Syriac, but that they are original Coptic poems composed on the model of these Greek hymns.[26]

---

[24] The Book of the Holy Mass, pp. 688-689.
[25] *Ibid.*, pp. 722-726; see also 1 Cor. 5:7, John 19:30, Matt. 27:50 and Matt. 28:5.
[26] Cf. De Lacy O'Leary, *The Daily Office and Theotokia of the Coptic Church* (London, 1911), pp. 53-57. See also Yassa Abdel-Messih.

Here below the incipits and explicits, in transliteration of Coptic texts from the *"Al-Absalmudiah as-Sanawiya al-Mukaddasah"* (Cairo, 1908) of C. Labib and from the *"Al-Absalmudiyat al-Mukaddasah as-Sanawiyat"* (Alexandria, 1908) of Mina al-Baramousi. English translation of the texts given below is from De Lacy O'Leary, "The Daily Office and Theotokia of the Coptic Church" (London, 1911).

a) *De Lacy O'Leary, p. 122*
   Theotokion of Sunday:
   "It was the symbol of God the Word, (Who became man) without separation. There is One from Two undefiled Deity is undivided, Consubstantial with the Father. And pure humanity without carnal intercourse Consubstantial with us according to nature."

b) *De Lacy O'Leary, p. 153*
   Theotokion of Monday:
   "He who has been is He who will be; He who came comes again, Jesus Christ the Word made flesh without change of substance was perfect man. He does not destroy or disturb or divide in any way as concerns the unity. . . . But is the same nature, the same substance, the same person, that is God the Word."

c) *De Lacy O'Leary, op. cit., p. 158*
   Theotokion of Tuesday:
   "She bore to us God the Word Who became man for our salvation. After He became man, He was still God, therefore She Who bore Him remained virgin."
   Op. cit., p. 159: "And again thus He took flesh in her without change of substance, a reasonable body Consubstantial with us, perfectly complete, at one with His mother, a soul supernal." He remained God continuously, and became perfect man.

d) *De Lacy O'Leary, op. cit., p. 166*
   Theotokion of Wednesday:
   "Hail workshop of undivided unity of natures brought together at one time without confusion. . . . For the fleshless has taken flesh and the Word is incarnate, the one without beginning commences life, the timeless enters time. The incomprehensible is comprehended, the unseen is seen, the Son of Living God becomes Son of Man in truth. Jesus Christ yesterday and today, He is, He is for ever, in the dispensation of unity let us praise and glorify Him."

116   *Does Chalcedon Divide or Unite?*

e) *De Lacy O'Leary, op. cit., p. 173*
   Theotokion of Thursday:
   "The one word itself begotten before the ages in Divine manner without body of the one Father. And this same One again was begotten in bodily form without change or detriment through his mother."
   Op. cit., p. 174: "For He is truly God, He became man without essential change; glory is due to Him henceforth for ever. For He Who was begotten as God, passionless from the Father, was begotten again as to the flesh, passionless from the virgin. There is one, out of two, Deity and humanity; thus the Magi worshipped Him and silently adored[27] Him."

The translation of the passage taken from Labib, p. 805, is given by De Lacy O'Leary, *op. cit.* p. 134.

   (God our Saviour). "He was with us by dispensation, Consubstantial with us as regards humanity. He was Consubstantial with God the Father as regards the essence of His Deity. There is one from two, deity and humanity, hypostatically united."

VII. IN THE TROPARION AND HYMNS:

1. The well known Troparion which is sung in both Coptic and Greek Churches from Easter till the Feast of the Ascension.[28]
   "Christ is risen from the death, by death having trampled upon death, and hath bestowed Life upon those in the tombs."

2. The hymn which was composed in the sixth century[29] which is recited in both churches.

---

[27] This statement agrees generally with the belief of St. John Damascene († 756 A.D.) (*Expositio Fidei*), P.G. col. 431: "Confiteor itaque Jesus Christum Dominum Nostrum, unam esse hypostasim, duasque naturas in ejus hypostasi unitas." "I confess, moreover, that Jesus Christ our Lord, is one by hypostasis (i.e. Person) and that there are Two Natures united in His hypostasis."

[28] In the Coptic Church it is recited in Greek, then in Coptic "Khristos aftonf" and finally in Arabic. Both the Coptic and the Arabic versions are literal translations from the Greek.

[29] Cf. King (Archdale, A.), *The Rites of Eastern Christendom*, Vol. II (Tipografia Poliglotta Vaticana, 1947), p. 164 says: "The Monogenes has been ascribed to the Emperor Justinian between the years 535 and 536, but it was more probably composed by Severus of Antioch (512-536). This statement has been confirmed by Ignace Ephrem II Rahmani, *Les Liturgies Orientales et Occidentales* (Mont Liban, 1924), p. 207, who says, 'The Greeks ascribed this hymn to Justinian the king and the Syrian (assuriani), the Jacobites, attributed it to their patriarch Severus (Sawira).'"

"Only-begotten Son and Word of God, Who being Immortal, yet didst deign for our salvation to be incarnate through our most holy Lady and Ever-Virgin Mary and without change didst become man and was crucified, by death having trampled upon death, do Thou Christ our God, save us, Thou, Who art One in the Holy Trinity and art glorified with the Father and the Holy Spirit."

3. The Troparia of the Canonical Hours of Sext and None occur in both Churches.[30]

a) *Office of Sext:*

"O Thou Who on the sixth day, at the Sixth Hour, wast nailed to the Cross because of the sin which Adam dared to commit in the garden," etc.[31]

"O Jesus Christ our God, Who wast nailed to the Cross at the Sixth Hour, Thou hast slain sin by the Word and hast given life to the dead, even to man, whom Thou didst create with Thy hands and who was dead through sin. Slay our passions by Thy saving and life-giving sufferings; and by the nails wherewith Thou wast nailed, preserve our minds from hurt of carnal works and worldly lusts," etc. [32]

"Thou hast wrought salvation in the midst of the earth, O Christ our God, in the stretching forth of Thy Holy Hands upon the Cross."[33]

"Thou wast pleased to ascend the Cross, that Thou mightest save those whom Thou didst create, from the slavery of enemy."[34]

b) *Office of None:*

"O Thou Who didst taste death in the flesh at the Ninth Hour for our sakes, slay our carnal lusts, O Christ our God, and save us."

"O Thou Who didst give the spirit into the hands of the Fa-

---

[30] These troparia have been edited by O. H. E. Khs- Burmester, "The Canonical Hours in the Coptic Church," *Orientalia Christiana Periodica,* Vol. 2 (1936), pp. 84-93.
[31] *Op. cit.,* p. 84.
[32] *Op. cit.,* p. 85.
[33] O. H. E. Khs-Burmester, *op. cit.,* p. 85.
[34] *Op. cit.,* p. 86.

ther. Thou didst hang upon the Cross about the Ninth Hour."[35]

"O Thou Who wast born of the Virgin for our sakes and didst bear the Cross, O Thou Good One, Thou didst slay death by Thy death, and didst manifest forth the resurrection by Thy resurrection."[36]

"When the thief saw the Creator hanging upon the Cross, he spake saying: If He Who is crucified with us were not an Incarnate God, the Sun would not have hidden its light, neither would the earth quake and tremble," etc.[37]

4. The following passages are taken from the Oktoichos Stichira, composed by St. John Damascene († 765 A.D.). These passages were accepted by the Copts, since they agree with their dogma. The Greek text is given according to the edition of 1855, p. 632 (Sunday in the Eighth Air) and the Coptic text is taken from the following manuscripts:

a) MS. No. 152, Lit. Library of the Coptic Patriarchate, Cairo foll. 94r-96v (new numeration 84r-82v,[38] which is entitled "Pikanon emmahshmen").

b) MS. No. 50, Lit. Library of the Coptic Patriarchate, Cairo foll. 108r-110r (new numeration 33r-32r).[39]

c) MS. No. 161, Lit. Library of the Coptic Patriarchate, Cairo foll. 184r-185r. (new numeration 4r-3r).[40]

d) MS. No. 115 Lit. Library of the Church of the Virgin Mary in Harat Zuwailah, foll. 31r-32r.[41]

e) The passages are found also in R. Tukhi's Euchologion of the Three Anaphorae, Rome A.M. 1452 (A.D. 1736) p. 248.

---

[35] *Op. cit.*, p. 93 reference only; for full text cf. John, Marquess of Bute, "The Coptic Morning Service for the Lord's Day," pp. 149-50.

[36] O. H. E. Khs-Burmester, *op. cit.*, p. 93, reference only; for full text, cf. John, Marquess of Bute, p. 150.

[37] O.H.E. Khs-Burmester, *op. cit.*, p. 93, reference only; for full text, cf. John, Marquess of Bute, *op. cit.*, p. 151.

[38] For the description of this MS. cf. Simaika Pasha, Catalogue etc., Vol. II, No. 756, p. 344.

[39] *Op. cit.*, No. 716, p. 327.

[40] *Op. cit.*, No. 982, p. 439.

[41] This MS. is dated on folio 140 (r): 7 Kiyahk A.M. 1394 (A.D. 1777).

Translation of the Greek Text

O Lord, though Thou didst stand in Judgement being judged by Pilate, yet Thou didst not leave the Throne being seated with the Father, and Thou didst rise from the dead and dist set free 'the world from the slavery of the enemy, as Compassionate One and Lover of man.

O Lord, Thou hast given us the Cross as a weapon against the Devil, for he shudders and trembles, not bearing to look upon the power, because It raised the dead and abolished death. On account of this, we adore Thy burial and Thy rising again.

O Lord, although the Jews laid Thee in a tomb as one dead, yet, as a King who is sleeping, soldiers guarded Thee. And as the treasure of life they sealed Thee with a seal, yet Thou didst rise, and hast granted to our souls immortality.

Translation of the Coptic Text
The Eighth Canon

Lord, Lord, Lord, though Thou didst stand in the place of Judgement before Pilate, being mocked, yet Thou didst not leave Thy Throne (and) Thou wast seated with the Father and Thou didst rise from the dead, and didst set free the world from the slavery of the enemy, in order that Thou mightest save our souls. Glory, etc.

Lord, Lord, Lord, Thou hast given to us Thine own Cross, being a weapon against the Devil who trembles and fears, being unable to manifest himself, because he saw the powers which are in Thee, because Thou didst raise the dead and didst abolish death alone, in order that Thou mightest save souls. Now, etc.

Lord, Lord, Lord, though the Jews laid Thee in a tomb as one dead and sealed (it) upon Thee with a seal so as to guard the tomb (yet) Thou didst rise from the dead and didst set free the world from the slavery of the enemy, in order that Thou mightest save our souls. Now, etc.

We have to mention that the Pope Cyril, the 110th Coptic Patriarch (1853-1861) who was on very friendly terms with Kallinicus, the 101st Patriarch (A.D. 1858-1861) of the Greek Church introduced in the Hymnology of the Coptic Church many Hymns from the Greek Church, and they are still in use in the Coptic Church to the present day.

VIII. In the Mimars (Homilies):

On certain occasions, some homilies (mimars) are read including the Faith of the Church. This extract is part of the Arabic Text of a homily (mimar) of St. Athanasius the Apostolic.

"We confess that the Son of God was born eternally of the Father and was born for our salvation of Mary the Virgin, according to flesh, at the end of the ages, as the Divine Apostle teaches saying: 'When the fullness of time was come, God sent forth His Son born of a Woman' (Gal. IV:14). We confess that He is the same Son of God, and according to the Spirit and the Son of man according to flesh that He is One Son not of Two Natures the One to be adored and the One not to be adored, but One Nature of the Word of God made flesh."[42]

DISCUSSION: Concerning the paper of Dr. Hakim Amin

8. Comments on the paper presented by Bishop Samuel:

V. C. SAMUEL: One has to beware in the transference of terms in the presentation of a paper relating to the practices of the non-Chalcedonian Church. For example, on page 1, paragraph 2 in using one essence as *ousia* there is a mistranslation. The last sentence on page 11 is badly punctuated.

ROMANIDES: Can the term *theantropos* be expressed in Coptic?

KHELLA: *Theanthropos* is used as an adjective in Arabic. There is much difficulty in the transference of theological terminology from one language to another. The above paper has been translated from Arabic and not from Greek and therefore this makes it difficult to understand in parts.

---

[42] Mimar Athanasius the Apostolic, the Arabic text foll. 30.

THE CHRISTOLOGICAL DOGMA AND ITS TERMINOLOGY

THE REV. PROF. GEORGES FLOROVSKY

In Scripture we are faced with the mystery of Jesus Christ presented as an historical personality born of the blessed virgin Mary, being human in the full sense, taken by many for ordinary man who eventually suffered and died on the cross. The common picture of our Lord is of one fully human, displaying a glory which is a mystery. The true image of our Lord can only be depicted in a suprahistorical vision in an act of faith.

From the beginning there has been certain confusion about him. He has always been seen as something greater than his merely human appearance.

The mystery is described in the New Testament as a history of *kenosis* (which is also a Cyrilline term). It is the mystery of humiliation. In the early Church the main concern was with the full and true humanity of our Lord and this is stated in the epistles of St. John, who combines his emphasis as to the super-human character of Christ in the beginning of his Gospel, that is the divine logos becoming flesh, with his challenge in the first epistle to those who would not believe that the logos became flesh.

Distinction should be made between the *kerygma* of the Church and the philosophical terminology in terms of which it is apprehended. The concern of the *kerygma* is with the message of salvation to be announced, with the saving person of Christ. The terminology of theology is for clarifying the conceptual grasp of the message and the person of the Saviour. The Christological problem is thus integral to the message of salvation, and should always be considered in that context.

The christological dispute in the early Church was concerned mainly with the message of salvation. When we turn to early christological conceptions we always find them in a soteriological perspective. There are two different concepts of salvation linked with two different anthropological dispositions.

Anthropological minimalism: This is found in the preaching of Apollinaris who went so far as to suggest that of the whole human fabric the "nous" could not be saved. Only fragments of Apollinaris' teaching remain, however. The "nous" in man is so perverse that it could not be human. "Nous" for Apollinaris is related to his pessimistic conception of the human being and this affected his christological conceptions and Christ for him was the *logos* clothed only in the externals of human nature. The emphasis again is purely soteriological. In Apollinaris there is a very low evaluation of the human condition and of the predicament which could result from it. Anthropological minimalism leads to maximalism of the divine element in Christ.

Anthropological maximalism: This concept is effected by exterior conditions. This as well as opposition to it is found in the so-called Antiochene school which also opposed Apollinaris. The Nestorian Christ was seen to be a suitable redeemer for the Pelagian man. Nestorianism and Pelagianism are examples of anthropological maximalism. Man has not been destroyed by sin, he is only lost and needs a guide who may be only human. This human being can be the maximum human being evident in the Old Testament as the Messiah. In anthropological maximalism no high Christology is necessary.

This useful scheme of anthropological minimalism-maximalism can be taken as the core of terminological differences in the christological debate. Christ has been regarded by some modern authors as a redeemer and the incarnation at the same time regarded simply as an act only of redemption. But this thinking in the early centuries of the Church was only really clarified in the christological writing of Maximus the Confessor, where the incarnation is said to have been the original purpose of the divine venture of creation. The later problem was whether redemption could be said to be the only reason for the incarnation. Maximus developed a comprehensive scheme giving reason for creation, that reason being in the incarnation, and the christology of the Eastern Churches was affected by this thinking. In the period preceding Maximus soteriological maximalism and minimalism was always rooted in the concept of man. This soteriology could be absolute or relative. When we discuss events there can be misunderstandings and conflict about this and terms must always be clarified.

Archbishop William Temple once wrote that "Chalcedon marked the

The Christological Dogma and its Terminology 123

bankruptcy of Greek metaphysics." But the glory of Chalcedon represents a fundamental intuition. Chalcedon states that Christ is one being perfectly divine and perfectly human.

This is an expression of a certain intuition and vision of our Lord and the conviction of a soteriological issue is apparent at Chelcedon. Any lesser conviction would destroy the apostolic *kerygma* about our salvation.

It has been suggested that Cyril was interested neither in exact terminology nor in scholastic definitions. There are examples in which the term *physis* and adjectives related to it are used in a non-exact sense and objections have been presented at this level. It is suggested that *physis* is used to emphasize that Christ was truly man. Cyril was not concerned with terminology but with truth and more attention should be given to the soteriological intuition of Cyril.

Ancient Greek was an unfamiliar language to many of the early theologians and patristic texts were often read then as now unfortunately merely as texts and one can always be negligent about terms in texts. Dissertations have been written about single words, e.g. *hypostasis*. Terminological clarity must only arise out of necessity when dealing with christology. People have always tended to be rather indifferent to terminological exactitude in the understanding of texts.

The Chalcedonian definition provides no reason for embarrassment in emphasizing that Christ is fully human and fully divine. This was addressed against the language of the Antiochenes who endeavored to describe the unity of Christ in a minimalized anthropological form.

We are still imprisoned in the terminology of monophysitism and duophysitism. One must be clear what is implied in duophysitism, for there are two types of duophysitism, the symmetric type and the asymmetric type. The problem of terminology remains as long as ancient idioms are still used. The christological dispute was extended to errors and areas where the Greek language was not the main language. We must look at the languages of the non-Chalcedonian Churches much more closely. We must look at the psychological significance of the term "person," as it is used in different languages both ancient and modern. It must always be remembered that words don't of themselves express the ideas that are intended to be expressed.

What is important is to turn to the basic vision and conclusion of the early Church. If we look at documents through Nestorian eyes they can be Nestorian in content, and so on. Divergence initially came and still comes in the sphere of spiritual vision and not in language. This is why Western theologians find it difficult to understand Eastern theologians and this because they have a different vision. In conclusion we should not omit to discuss the metaphysical side and pay attention to spirituality. Anyone who insists in avoiding nature reduces man. The separation from the beginning will cease to be of importance when we cease to look at terminology and look at the life of the Churches instead.

DISCUSSION: Concerning the presentation of Prof. Florovsky

2. Comments on Professor Florovsky's presentation:

VERGHESE: Professor Florovsky's presentation proved to be illuminating and confirmed much of what has been thought for the past twenty years. The concern expressed was not merely with philosophical terminology, but with a genuine soteriological teaching. This came out particularly in the comments on anthropological minimalism and maximalism. The Professor also expressed a high view of man which requires a Chalcedonian Christology. Alexandrian Christology may be suspect that while in formula it accepts the full view of the divine-human Christ, nevertheless that it does not take man as seriously as it should. The fear of the non-Chalcedonians is not against the Eastern Orthodox Church but against the Orthodoxy of the interpretation of Chalcedon in the Western Churches. The concept of *theosis* which is deeply centered in the theology of the Eastern Churches is not as deeply centered in the theology of the Churches of Western Christendom. There is a gap between God and man in Western theology. Chalcedonian theology seems to us to emphasize the gap. For man to grow into the fullness of God can only be realized when it is seen that God has achieved fullness of man's vocation to be the image of God in the man Jesus Christ.

V. C. SAMUEL: It is good that Professor Florovsky places more emphasis on the spiritual rather than on the terminological problem. In fact, the agreement in faith between our two traditions can be found only there. But if we go on to say, as some English scholars like H. M. Relton has done, that Chalcedon was opposed by monks in Egypt for whom Jesus Christ could not have been our brother, we shall be absolutely wrong in our assessment. For even the statement that "Christ was our brother" has been insisted on by the men accepted as teachers by the non-Chalcedonian side including Dioscorus.

ROMANIDES: Father Florovsky has presented to us the key to the problems facing this consultation, namely the question of the inseparable relation which exists between dogma and spirituality.

In this regard I would emphasize that the spirituality of such Alexandrian theologians as St. Athanasius and St. Cyril and St. Anthony the Great and the Great Macarius of Egypt is not essentially different from that of such Cappadocians as St. Basil the Great, St. Gregory of Nyssa, St. Gregory the Theologian and St. Maximus the Confessor. It is in this basic identity in spirituality rooted in the Biblical understanding of grace in terms of glorification or theosis that we should approach the common ground of dogma of our two essentially identical earlier traditions and then work toward a descriptice analysis of any ensuing divergences.

I would strongly suggest that the doctrine of God and His revelation to the prophets and apostles be put at the center of our deliberations since these are the key to spirituality which in turn is the core of man's understanding of God and His relation to man, especially by means of the Incarnation. I developed this theme in my study on Theodore of Mopsuestia and I believe that it was there decisively shown that the heretical foundations of Nestorianism, as well as of Arianism and Dynamic Monarchianism, are to be found in a wrong understanding of God's relation to creation which automatically comes about when Biblical apophatic theology, which is common to both our traditions, is lacking. It is my opinion that the general abandonment of Biblical apophaticism by the Latin tradition is the root cause of the Roman Catholic and some Protestant propensity toward Nestorianism, as well as of an incorrect approach to the doctrines of grace and salvation.

It is interesting to note how the very same definitions concerning God's relation to creation are to be found in dynamic Monarchianism, Arianism and Nestorianism and also how Apollinaris was attacked by the Cappadocians not only for his heretical Christology and soteriology, but also for his doctrine of the Holy Trinity.

I suggest then that we must complete our discussions concerning Christology by a careful examination of our understanding of God, His relation to creation, and man's theosis. I suspect that in uncovering traditional unanimity in this area we will be better prepared to break through our terminological divergences and the suspicions which have lurked behind them for so many centuries.

BOROVOY: The comment of Verghese on the unity of the Chalcedonian and non-Chalcedonian Churches in the concept of theosis and that Western Christians ignore this concept of theosis, is open to objection. Man is the object of theosis and no one can doubt that this is so whether in Western or Eastern theology. In Western theology also man is saved so that he might come to theosis. Spirituality in striving for theosis can forget about the man and manhood and this is true also about much of the spirituality of the Eastern Churches. In Russian theology we have an excellent book by Professor Popov about the idea of theosis in the teaching of St. Athanasius the Great. In general a heretic is not a person who makes mistakes but is a Christian who puts his personal interpretation of his beliefs against the teaching of the Church when the Church has clearly expressed its judgment on his mistakes through Ecumenical Councils or by other appropriate means.

KONIDARIS: It was excellent to note how the Testament was used by Florovsky. Christian dogma should be expressive of the New Testament teachings on Christ. In the third century the Antiochenes emphasized the humanity of Christ. The rationalism of this type of thinking has never been fully dealt with. The tradition of Alexandria about the *logos* as it appears in St. John's Gospel was one building on the teaching of Philo about the nature of the *logos*. Endeavor was made in this school to achieve a full understanding of the *logos*. At the same time the question of the divinity of Christ was dealt with excellently. As St. Athanasius expressed the purpose of incarnation, God became man that we might become divine. The extremists of Alexandria who disregard the human element in Christ have been called monophysites. In the same connection the contribution of the Cappadocians to trinitarian thinking must be commended.

After the death of Cyril there was general disunion on the matter of the unity of Christ.

It might be that in our time we should evolve a new terminology in regard to christology. The terminology of the Fourth Ecumenical Council did help in clarifying christology. We nowadays have to distinguish between the Alexandrian school of theology and catholic theology, as evidenced particularly in the Ancient Church.

Nissiotis: Both anthropology and theosis have been mentioned and these are profound roots which affect our understanding of man. No one has ever questioned the nature of God as we question it today.

Can we deny that we live in an era of the church event? This fact has possibly been disregarded by the Eastern Orthodox Churches, which Churches need to work out this problem bearing in mind what Professor Torrence has said in another context, that is that "all ecclesiologies depend on christological dogma."

Because of diminishing interest in christology, ecclesiology is shaken and is becoming more and more difficult. Torrence has classified church doctrine following a christological approach. He sees in the Roman Catholic Church divine monophysitism, with the Pope being equivalent to Christ. The Orthodox and the Ancient Oriental Churches have a common ecclesiological approach. It is interesting to note the second and third chapters of the document De Ecclesia of the Second Vatican Council which betray a duophysite tendency.

The Reformed tradition of Western Christianity fights against schematic duophysitism going more to humanity than to divinity in its theologizing.

Ecclesiology should be of first importance to us in our thinking of this and our subsequent consultations.

Bishop Samuel: We have discussed many matters widely but let us think of our people and give something practical where they can understand our discussion of the difficulties.

Damaskinos: It is not by chance that monophysitism arose in places where Greek was not the native language. The Chalcedonian formulations were only well known up to the sixth century in the Churches of Chalcedon and only after that date in the Oriental Churches. Prior to the sixth century, there was more Alexandrian understanding, and this should have prepared the ground for the understanding of Chalcedon. Through the writings of many theologians words such as *hypostasis, physis* and *ousia* passed into Armenian for example quite incorrectly by reason of inadequate translation of the relevant documents of the Fourth Ecumenical Council; also, in post-Chalcedonian writings, for example in citing the definition of Chalcedon, the term "asygchytos" = (arm.) "anspho theli" is given as (arm.) "ancharneli" = "amigos." Thus and by reason of national historical factors that Council was understood by some of the Ancient Oriental Churches as being Nestorian.

ECCLESIOLOGICAL ISSUES CONCERNING THE RELATION OF EASTERN ORTHODOX AND ORIENTAL ORTHODOX CHURCHES

METROPOLITAN PAULOS MAR GREGORIOS

In a perceptive paper presented at the Bristol Conversations in July 1967, Professor Gerasimos Konidaris drew attention to the position of the Orthodox Churches in communion with Constantinople on "The Inner Continuity and Coherence of Trinitarian and Christological dogma in the seven ecumenical councils".

What was most interesting in his treatment was the division of the Seven Councils into two parts. Nicea (325) and Constantinople (381) belong to the first part - the latter especially was a positive achievement of the "Greek-Christian" spirit in clarifying the Trinitarian and Christological dogmas. The symbol of the faith is now finalized; no further changes are to be effected.

The five later councils including Ephesus (431), Chalcedon (451) and the three subsequent ones, belong to a different class. They regard the symbol of the first two councils as unchangeable. Their task is to further elucidate it, not to reformulate the symbol as was finalized in the perfect Greek of St. Gregory of Nyssa in 381.

This insight of Professor Konidaris is of central significance for the relation between our two churches. We can all agree that the formulations of Nicea and Constantinople have a unique and final quality which it is safest not to tamper with.

These documents were prepared by fathers who are common to our Churches. They were not all necessarily Greeks by ethnic origin or nationality. It is important to point this out. Most of these fathers came from the Churches of Africa and Asia, from what later became the Patriarchates of Alexandria and Antioch. The chief among the fathers of the three councils, Athanasius and Cyril of Alexandria and the Cappodocians came from Egypt or Asia Minor. There is no reason to claim that only the Greek church understood them and their terminology. The literate peoples of Asia and Africa were at least as capable of using Greek terminology as Indians and Americans are capable of using English terminology today.

But the more important point is the inviolable character of the formulation of faith of the first two ecumenical synods. Once this point is adequately grasped by the two sides, some of our ecclesiological differences become capable of resolution.

Historically speaking the question then is what did the third Ecumenical Council, i.e. of Ephesus (431) do, and what did the Council of Chalcedon (451) do, in relation to the first two councils?

In the case of the Third Council, there was a clear heresy against which the council proclaimed itself - that attributed to Nestorius, Archbishop of Constantinople. The Alexandrian Church led the attack against this heresy as in the case of the Arian heresy more than a century earlier.

They condemned Nestorius and the heresy ascribed to him that in Christ there are two distinct **prosopa**, two distinct persons - one human and one divine. Whether Nestorius taught this or not, it is a heresy, and the Church still condemns this teaching. In this sense the decision of the Third Council is of high doctrinal value, and clarifies the creed of Nicea-Constantinople.

The case of the Fourth Council seems to be different in several ways. In the first place, the heresy for which the Council of Chalcedon was held in order to combat is still unknown. If it was to condemn the doctrine of Eutyches, we neither know what Eutyches taught nor who followed him in his teaching. On the assumption, however, that there was a heretical teaching which held that the human nature of Christ was not consubstantial with ours, or that it was absorbed by his divine nature, those who accept Chalcedon and those who reject that council agree that Christ is consubstantial with us in his humanity and that the human nature with all its properties and faculties remains distinct and unabsorbed in Christ. We also agree in condemning Eutyches on the assumption that he denied the double consubstantiality. It is clear that on the non-Chalcedonian side we do not do this on the authority of the Council of Chalcedon.

It is because our own tradition is authentic and true that we affirm the double consubstantiality and the united divine-human nature of Christ. We are happy that both those Orthodox churches in communion with Constantinople and even our Roman Catholic friends accept this double consubstantiality. In this respect all of us adhere to the one authentic tradition, even when some of us do not accept the council of Chalcedon. This means that for us Chalcedon is not an essential element of the authentic tradition, and as far as we are concerned, other churches can also reject Chalcedon and still be in the authentic tradition.

This is not so with the Third Council. The Church of the East rejects the Third Council of Ephesus (431). As a result, Nestorius as well as Theodore and Diodore, whose teachings have been condemned by the authentic tradition, continue to be operative in the church of the East. If the Churches of our non-Chalcedonian family were now to seek communion with the Church of the East, the acceptance of the Third Council, or at least the major teachings of that council, would be a necessary condition. The Theotokos formula and the one prosopon formula would also have to be insisted upon. If these doctrines are accepted, we may not insist on their acceptance of the Third Council, but would find our unity on the basic of the Kerygma of Nicea and Constantinople supplemented by a formal repudiation of the two-prosopa doctrine and by the affirmation of the Theotokos formula as well as a Christology of the hypostatic union.

This basic difference between the nature of Ephesus 431 and Chalcedon 451 needs to be further discussed among our churches. The reason why we have not included the Church of the East in these meetings - the only oriental church to be so kept out of our conversations - is simply that there are real Christological differences between both, while among ourselves we find basic agreement about our Christological positions. It is not inconceivable that extended theological conversations with the Church of the East will reveal that they too affirm the hypostatic union of the two natures in Christ, and thereby do in fact affirm the single proposopon, and that Mary was truly the bearer of the God-Man.

If this were to be the case, then the Third Council as such need not be an obstacle, though condemnation of those heresies condemned by Ephesus 431 may still be necessary to restore communion between us.

It is because some of us have now become convinced that in affirming the two natures of Christ, the Chalcedonian

Orthodox Churches also affirm the hypostatic union and all the "four adverbs", that we are no longer afraid of pursuing further the possibility of restoring communion between our two families of Churches. Professor Tsonievsky of the Bulgarian church was basically right in referring to "the non-Chalcedonian fear"... "that the Orthodox (i.e. Chalcedonian) Church has departed somewhat from the decisions of the Third Ecumenical Council against Nestorius and that it has introduced certain Nestorian elements into the faith"(1). This fear was actually there and is only now being dispelled; just as is the fear also on the Chalcedonian side that we who stand firmly on the Three ecumenical councils, in rejecting the council of Chalcedon, were affirming something less than the full human nature in Christ.

It is now possible for us to do what Professor Tsonievsky asked us to do, namely that we "must stop accusing the Council of Chalcedon of Nestorianism", especially if we take Chalcedon as corrected by the Fifth Council and its interpretation of Chalcedon.

We can also agree that even the Chalcedonian churches should not separate the Fourth Council from the Fifth. We are not able to say, however, that the Sixth and Seventh Councils of the Chalcedonians are organically or integrally related either to the Fourth and Fifth or to the first three. It was the Fifth Council that could dispel our doubts about the Fourth. For in first refusing to condemn the teachings of Theodore, Theodoret and Ibas, the Roman church at least among the Chalcedonians gave ground to our suspicion that Chalcedon actually did have some Nestorian implications. It took quite a bit of time for Pope Vigilius to accept the Fifth council. If the Decretal epistle of Vigilius (2) is genuine, the Pope admits he was wrong in defending the Three Chapters. It is such kind of defence of the Three Chapters and of teachers like Theodore, Theodoret and Ibas by a large section of those supporting Chalcedon, that made Chalcedon itself suspect. It is also a historical fact that despite the retractions of Pope Vigilius (554/ 555) and the confirmation by his successor Pelagius I of the Acts of the Fifth Council, that council was bitterly opposed in the whole of Northern Italy, in England, France and Spain, and also in parts of Africa and Asia. Milan was in schism until 571 when the Henoticon was published. In Istria the schism continued for a century and a half (3). Even today opinions crop up in western theological manuals which give rise to fears that Nestorianism is still not quite dead among the western Chalcedonians.

The Third Council of Constantinople, called the sixth Ecumenical (680-681), enumerated in its decree and "piously gave its full assent to the five holy and Ecumenical Synods". This decree also specifies the particular heresy or heretic against which each council is convened: Chalcedon was against "Eutyches and Dioscurus, hated of God", while the Fifth Council was against "Theodore of Mopsuestia, Origen, Didymus, Evagrius, and the writings of Theodoret against the Twelve Chapters of the celebrated Cyril, and the Epistile... by Ibas".

We were not there, the non-Chalcedonians. If we were, we would probably have liked to find out what was the heresy of "Dioscurus, hated of God". Until we find out, there can be no question of our accepting the sixth council as being in any sense in the right tradition. The condemnation of Didymus and Evagrius must be for their Origenism. That is a question which we need to examine further. There is a whole series of people condemned by the sixth council for their supposedly Monothelete views - Theodorus of Pharan, Sergius, Pyrrhus, Paul, Peter, Pope Honorius, Cyrus of Alexandria, Macarius of Antioch and Stephen. They are accused of affirming "one will and operation in the two natures of Christ our true God". I am not sure which is the true heresy to which these men adhered - that of "two natures" or of "one will and operation". Their heresy is regarded as being "similar to the mad and wicked doctrine of the impious Apollinaris, Severus and Themistius". Putting Apollinaris and Severus in the same bracket shows how little their thought was understood by the sixth synod. Themistius of Alexandria on the other hand so strongly affirmed the humanity of Christ as to attribute ignorance of certain matters to the human soul of Christ.

If acceptance of the Sixth council thus means our agreeing to condemn Dioscurus and Severus, who are true teachers of the Authentic tradition, then we must choose the two fathers mentioned in preference to the Sixth council which appears to us badly muddled, not to say in grievous error.

Its **horos** or dogmatic definition we find interesting. The first part of this **horos** reads: "Our Lord Jesus Christ must be confessed to be very God and very man, one of the holy and consubstantial and life-giving Trinity, perfect in Deity and perfect in humanity, very God and very man, of a reasonable soul and human body subsisting; consubstantial with the Father as touching his Godhead and consubstantial with us as touching his manhood; in all things like unto us, sin only excepted; begotten of his Father before all ages according to his Godhead, but in these last days for us men and for our salvation made man of the Holy Ghost and of the Virgin Mary, strictly and properly the Mother of God according to the flesh; one and the same Christ our Lord, the only-begotten Son, of two natures unconfusedly, unchangeably, inseparably, indivisibly to be recognized, the peculiarities of neither nature being lost by the union but rather the proprieties of each nature being preserved, concurring in one Person and in one subsistence, not parted or divided into two persons but one and the same only-begotten Son of God, the Word, our Lord Jesus Christ, according as the Prophets of old have taught us and as our Lord Jesus Christ himself hath instructed and the creed of the holy Fathers hath delivered to us."

This we find basically acceptable, though not as a formula of confession like or instead of the Niceno-Constantinopolitan **pistis**.

The second part is of a different kind, and needs separate examination. "We likewise declare that in him are two natural wills and two natural operations, indivisibly, inconvertibly, inseparably, inconfusedly, according to the teaching of the holy Fathers. And these two natural wills are not contrary the one to the other (God forbid!) as the impious heretics assert, but his human will follows and that not as resisting and reluctant, but rather as subject to his divine and omnipotent will. For it was right that the flesh should be moved but subject to the divine will, according to the most wise Athanasius. For as his flesh is called and is the proper will of God the Word, as he himself says: "I came down from heaven, not that I might do mine own will but the will of the Father which sent me!" where he calls his own will the will of his flesh, inasmuch as his flesh was also his own. For as his most holy and immaculate animated flesh was not destroyed because it was deified but continued in its own state and nature, so also his human will, although deified, was not suppressed, but was rather preserved according to the saying of Gregory Theologus: 'His will (i.e. the Saviour's) is not contrary to God but altogether deified.'

"We glorify two natural operations indivisibly, immutably, inconfusedly, inseparably in the same our Lord Jesus Christ our true God, that is to say a divine operation and a human operation, according to the divine preacher Leo, who most distinctly asserts as follows: "For each form does in communion with the other what pertains properly to it, the Word, namely, doing that which pertains to the Word, and the flesh that which pertains to the flesh.

"For we will not admit one natural operation in God and in the creature as we will not exalt into the divine essence what is created, nor will we bring down the glory of the divine nature to the place suited to the creature."

Here, as earlier in the decree, the Tome of Leo is expressly affirmed. The decree actually calls the Tome "the pillar of the right faith". You can perhaps understand that all this is rather difficult for us to accept. For us Leo is still a heretic. It may be possible for us to refrain from condemning him by name, in the interests of restoring communion between us. But we can not in good conscience accept the Tome of Leo as "the pillar of the right faith" or accept a council which made such a declaration. The council approves explicitly what I clearly regard as heresy in the Tome of Leo "Each form does in communion with the other what pertains properly to it, the Word, namely doing that which pertains to the Word, and the flesh that which pertains to the flesh" (4). If one rightly understands the hypostatic union, it is not possible to say that the flesh does something on its own, even if it is said to be in union with the Word. The flesh does not have its own hypostasis. It is the hypostasis of the Word which acts through the flesh. It is the same hypostasis of the Word which does the actions of the Word and of his own flesh.

The argument in the horos of this Sixth council is basically unacceptable to us. The reason it gives for not admitting one natural operation in Christ which is both divine and human, proceeding from the divine and human natures of the same hypostasis, is that they would "not exalt into the divine essence what is created, nor... bring down the glory of the divine nature to the place suited to the creature".

One can understand the first part of this objection, though not the conclusion drawn from it. The creature is not to participate in the divine **ousia**, but only in the uncreated **energeia** of the Divine essence. But in Jesus Christ, man the creature is united to the divine person or hypostasis. If we deny that, we are not Christians. The operation of the incarnate Logos is a divine-human energeia and we cannot say that it was only the flesh or the human nature that was crucified. **They crucified the Lord of Glory.** What is the point of saying: "We will not bring down the glory of the divine nature to the place suited to the creature", unless the Sixth council wanted to deny the incarnation itself?

It seems to us that the Sixth council was much more based on the Tome of Leo than on the writings of St. Cyril. Where it is based on Cyrilline teaching, it is acceptable, as for example, where it says both the miracles and the sufferings were performed by one entity, Christ our true God who became man. We are unable to say what this council says when it affirms "two wills and two operations concurring most fitly in him". We are not sure that "each nature wills and does the things proper to it", for we believe that it is the hypostasis of Christ who wills and operates through his divine-human nature. The natures have no subsistence of their own apart from the hypostasis who operates in both natures. We would thus prefer to speak of the one incarnate nature of the Logos, both divine and human natures united in the one hypostasis of the Logos, with a divine-human will and operation.

* * *

To summarise: Acceptance of the Sixth Council is much more difficult for us than the acceptance of Chalcedon. The following are the chief reasons:

a) Quite apart from the fact that our own fathers were not present at this council, we observe that this council explicitly and unjustifiedly condemns our fathers Dioscurus and Severus, and calls the former "hated of God", and the doctrine of the latter "mad and wicked" (5).

b) We are unable to accept the dithelete formula, attributing will and energy to the natures rather than to the hypostasis. We can only affirm the one united and unconfused divine-human nature, will and energy of Christ the incarnate Lord.

c) We find that this Sixth council exalts as its standard mainly the teaching of Leo and Agatho, popes of Rome, paying only lip-service to the teachings of the Blessed Cyril. We regard Leo as a heretic for his teaching that the will and operation of Christ is to be attributed to the two natures of Christ rather than to the one hypostasis. The human nature is as "natural" to Christ the incarnate Word as is the divine. It is one hypostasis who now is both divine and human, and all the activities come from the one hypostasis. We therefore insist on the one theandric nature, will and energy of Christ the Incarnate Lord, and condemn the teachings of Leo. We cannot therefore accept the horos of the Sixth council based on the teachings of Leo. This subject of course deserves further and more detailed study.

CONCLUSION

This paper has been written subject to correction by my learned brethren on the Chalcedonian and non-Chalcedonian sides. Its implications are quite serious. If the restoration of communion between our two families of Churches were to be dependent on our acceptance of the four councils now rejected by the non-Chalcedonian family, then we have little reason at present to hope that this condition can be fulfilled. If this is the **conditio sine qua non** in the minds of theologians on the non-Chalcedonian side, we would like to be told so, in order that we may communicate this to the holy synods of our churches and await further instruction from them as to whether we continue our bi-lateral conversations. My own view would be that we should so continue, because despite our basic disagreement on this point of the four councils, we do still have so much in common, and we have a significant contribution to make together as Eastern Orthodox Churches to the world-wide ecumenical discussion.

On the other hand, if we take seriously the valuable insight of Professor Konidaris, that the formulations of the First and Second Councils are of a decisive character, and later councils are to be seen only as exegetical to the meaning of the faith of Nicea and Constantinople, then it is possible for us to recommend to our parent churches to begin formal conversations with a view to restoring communion between our two families. The following is proferred as a basis or starting point for such conversations:

1. In a substantially common statement, to be formally declared by the Holy Episcopal Synods of all the autocephalous churches, with any necessary changes to suit the condition of each Church, we should state clearly that we

share, between our two families, substantially the same authentic tradition of the undivided Christian church in relation to our understanding of and teaching on the Blessed and Holy Trinity, the Incarnation of our Lord Jesus Christ, the procession and activity of the Holy Spirit, the nature of the Church and the place of the blessed Virgin Mary, the saints and all the faithful departed in it, the nature of the ministry and sacraments in the Church, and our expectation of the world to come with the advent in glory of our Lord and the resurrection of the dead.

2. This common statement would also include a page on our common Christology, emphasizing mainly those things which we have in common, but also speaking of our different formulations in regard to nature, will and energy in our Lord Jesus Christ. It would be stated that variety in forms of worship, language and culture, and in formulations of faith can within certain prescribed limits serve to enrich rather than impoverish the common tradition of the church.

3. The statement would also make clear that while it is not possible for the Chalcedonian Churches to repudiate or reject any of the seven councils, it is equally difficult for the non-Chalcedonians now to formally accept the fourth, fifth, sixth and seventh councils recognized by the Chalcedonian family. It could be made clear that the non-Chalcedonians would refrain from formally condemning either the council of Chalcedon or Pope Leo. The statement will also make clear that the Chalcedonian churches would refrain from condemning Dioscurus and Severus as heretics. It could also be made clear that our two families agree in condemning the teachings of both Nestorius and Eutyches as heretical.

4. The statement would also say that at least for the time being, the jurisdictions would remain distinct on the basis of the different liturgical traditions, e.g. the two Patriarchates of Antioch and Alexandria, as well as of Constantinople could continue with their different jurisdictions. The hope should be expressed in the statement that as mutual confidence grows between the various liturgical traditions a reorganization of the jurisdictions would become possible. Clear assurances can be given to certain churches that entering into communion with another church will not violate its administrative or jurisdictional integrity.

* * *

The next immediate step is the appointment of a Joint Commission by the two families, who will meet officially and work out the statement along the suggested lines. The standing committee of the Oriental Orthodox Churches has already been so authorized to act on behalf of the Oriental Orthodox Churches. As soon as similar action is announced by the churches of the Chalcedonian family, we could proceed to the convening of a joint meeting of the two commissions. One of our jobs here at the present meeting would be to prepare an agenda for the joint meeting, and to nominate a small group of people who will be prepared to assist in the organization of the joint meeting.

I even venture to suggest that the first meeting of the Joint Commission should be held in January 1971 in Addis Ababa.

Footnotes
1. Bristol Report p. 179
2. **Patrologia Latina (Migne) Tome LXIX Col. 122 sqq.**
3. See note in **The Nicene and Post Nicene Fathers**, Series Two, Volume XIV, p. 323.
4. **"agit enim utraque forma cum alterius communione quod proprium est; Verbo scilicet operante quod Verbi est, et carne exequente quod carnis est."**
5. Severus is also called "God-hated" in the letter of the Sixth Council to the Pope Agatho.

ECCLESIOLOGICAL ISSUES INHERENT IN THE RELATIONS BETWEEN EASTERN CHALCEDONIAN AND ORIENTAL NON-CHALCEDONIAN CHURCHES

PROF. JOHN D. ZIZIOULAS

I

The previous two unofficial consultations between Oriental and Eastern Orthodox Theologians (Aarhus, 1964 and Bristol, 1967) have shown that considerable progress has been made towards a better understanding of the theological problems which have divided the Eastern Chalcedonian and the Oriental non-Chalcedonian Churches for so many centuries. This progress is noteworthy especially insofar as it concerns fundamental Christological issues on the basis of which the separation of the two Churches has taken place and has been sustained for centuries. When one reads the minutes of the discussions at Aarhus, one is struck by the growing and unreserved enthusiasm of the participants in these discussions, as they discover that many of the basic differences in Christology, traditionally known as the reasons for separation, must be attributed to misunderstandings and that a remarkable measure of agreement has been discovered. This agreement is confirmed and clarified further at the Bristol meeting which discussed not only the fifth and sixth century Christological issues but also those aspects of Christology which have been underlined by the controversies concerning the two wills of Christ, and on which essential agreement was also discovered and proclaimed at this meeting (1). At the same meeting it was also felt that not only in Christology but also in matters which have not been studied particularly but were simply discussed in passing, such as anthropology, spirituality, liturgical life and the concept of the Church, the same measure of agreement seemed to exist (2).

With this discovery of theological agreement in mind the participants in the Bristol meeting felt that "it is a first priority for our Churches to explore with a great sense of urgency adequate steps to restore the full communion between our Churches, which has been sadly interrupted for centuries" (3). The basis of such a restoration of full communion would be "the formulation of a joint declaration in which we express together in the same formula our common faith in the One Lord Jesus Christ whom we all acknowledge to be perfect God and perfect Man" (4). Such a formula would not have the status of a confession of faith or of a creed and should be approved officially by the Churches (5).

It is undoubtedly right to seek the restoration of full communion between divided Christians on the basis of agreement on fundamental theological issues especially as these issues affect our salvation. But while this is true, this agreement should not be conceived in isolation from the entire life of the Church as it is expressed not only theoretically by the theologians but practically by the actual congregations, above all in their eucharistic life. The development and spread of confessionalism in the last centuries has led even the Orthodox to regard the differences between divided Christians as being mainly matters of theological or strictly speaking doctrinal disagreement, and to think of re-union as the automatic result of an agreement on these issues. This confessionalistic approach to the problem of healing existing schisms is basically incompatible with Orthodoxy. Genuine Orthodox tradition never allowed an understanding of the Church in confessional terms. Confession of faith in any form, written or oral, through creeds or through teaching and preaching, is only part of the reality of the Church, and receives its full and proper meaning only if it is placed in the contest of the living Church. In this context confession of faith becomes **Homologia** not just in the sense of a theological formulation of faith but of **martyria** which involves the Church's life at its best, as it is expressed in the Holy Eucharist (6).

This ecclesiological principle affects the methodology of healing schisms in a fundamental way. Achievement of re-union is not to be sought primarily through dialogue and negotiations of a confessional character. Sometimes such a dialogue may not bear fruit at all, and yet understanding and growth towards unity may develop through other channels of Church life. And even when such confessional dialogue does prove to be fruitful, unity should not and cannot be based simply on the results of such a dialogue. Schism and division do not affect only the Church's teaching. Even if a schism begins with confessional disturbance, it always affects much more deeply and widely the reality of the Church.

The necessity, therefore, of looking into the broader reality of the Church in order to see in what way it has been essentially affected by division, is inescapable in every attempt at healing a schism on the basis of Orthodox ecclesiology. We should bear in mind that the Oriental and Eastern Orthodox Churches have not simply been in disagreement on matters of Orthodox faith but in a **state of schism**. This is a very harsh reality, much harsher than any disagreement on issues of doctrine. The roots of this reality are deep and complicated and call for a very careful and delicate treatment of the problem.

In the lines that follow an attempt will be made to point out some of these complicated issues which are rooted in our schismatic situation. These issues will be placed in the light of Orthodox ecclesiology and tradition to see in what way they should be treated in order to bring us nearer to the healing of schism. Many, if not all, of these issues have already been mentioned at the Bristol Consultation as problems to be dealt with mainly on the practical level (7). The present paper is based on the assumption that these issues are far from being minor matters of practical arrangements, which should simply follow the great achievement of a common formula of faith. They represent real ecclesiological issues the discussion of which may prove to be so difficult at points as to lead to an impasse. We must, I think, be prepared to face such an impasse wherever it occurs and not try to heal a schism disregarding the ecclesiological implications of the measures we take.

II

Schism takes effect between two Churches when a break occurs in **communio in sacris**. Such a break, however, does not refer simply to the act of taking Holy Communion from the same Altar. This particular act of taking Holy Communion is only a detail, essential of course and of the highest importance, yet not the whole thing that makes up the reality of Eucharistic communion. Eucharistic communion is not simply an **act**, and the Body of Christ in which we partake through this communion is not simply an objective **thing** lying on the Holy Altar. The meaning of this communion as expressed by St. Paul calls our attention to a reality broader than this objectified Holy Sacrament: "The cup of blessing which we bless is it not a communion (**koinonia**) of the blood of Christ? The bread which we break is it not a communion of the Body of Christ? Because there is one bread, we who are many are one body, for we all partake of the one loaf" (I Cor. 10, 16-17). Eucharistic communion, placed in this perspective of St. Paul, is not only **communio in sacris** but also and at the same time **communio sanctorum**. The Early Church was from the beginning deeply conscious of this fact which decisively influenced her whole life and structure (8).

Every schism affects in one way or another this **communio sanctorum**. This was dramatically indicated in the Early Church by the practice of the crossing out from the **Diptychs** of the Liturgy, which took place whenever a schism occurred, and of the restoration in the same **Diptychs** of the names crossed out, after the schism was healed. The schism between Rome and the Eastern Patriarchates which took place in the early years of the fifth century because of the well-known events in the life of Chrysostom started with the crossing out of Chrysostom's name from the **Diptychs** of Constantinople, Alexandria and Antioch. The first act of healing this schism took place in Antioch when its Patriarch Alexander restored again the name of Chrysostom in the **Diptychs** in A.D. 413, i.e. **even while Chrysostom was no longer alive**. The importance which was attached to this act by the Early Church in connection with schism was so great that during the Acacian schism the Pope included in the well-known "Formula Horsmidae" anathemas not only against Nestorius, Eutyches, Dioscorus, Acacius, etc. but also against the successors of Acacius (Fravitas, Euphemius and Macedonius) not because of heresy but for the reason that they had kept Acacius' name in the **Diptychs** of Constantinople. The schism would be healed only when there was full identity between the Diptychs of Rome and those of Constantinople.

The meaning of the **Diptychs** cannot be understood outside the context of ecclesiology. Membership in the Church is in the last analysis communion not only with Christ but also with the "saints", i.e. with the community of the Church as a whole (9), including those "saints" that have already departed from this life. This communion is expressed in the

Eucharist with the commemoration of the heads of the various communities in the Anaphora right after the consecration when the celebrating bishop's name is "in the first place" mentioned aloud. The earliest form of such a commemoration in the ancient liturgies, namely the expression: "Remember, oh Lord, in the first place every Orthodox bishop" (10), indicates that all local communities are taking part in each Eucharist with all the saints, living and departed. The Eucharist is thus a real **synodos** of the Church of God (11) gathered together "from the ends of the earth", as the **Didache** saw it from early times (12). An oclusion from this company of the saints by means of crossing out certain names from the **Diptychs is thus to be understood ecclesiologically and not as a mere disciplinary act. The gravity which the ancient Church attached to anathema** lies precisely in the view that in each Eucharistic celebration the entire communion of the saints participates in God's Kingdom and an exclusion from this communion means a break of deep ecclesiological, soteriological and even eschatological significance (13).

This ecclesiological view to which, I am sure, both Oriental and Eastern Orthodox firmly adhere, shows that full communion in the Eucharist cannot be conceived without a complete identity in the communion of the "saints". The "saints" in the Orthodox tradition are not to be understood independently of their participation in the **communio sanctorum**. The original New Testament notion of the "saints" (plutal) should not be lost when one thinks of a particular "saint" (in the singular). The notion of "saint" is basically **ecclesiological**. There is no "canonization" of an individual on the basis of personal merits. The idea of "merit" is foreign to Orthodox tradition, and so is the practice of "canonization". A saint is with the guidance of the Holy Spirit **recognized** as such by the Church's consciousness and is **singled out** from the "saints" not in order to become objectively something in himself, but to serve as a **point of reference** to the **communio sanctorum** and through and in that to God in Christ for each member of the Church as he struggles in this fallen world to find and maintain his relationship with God. In this way the particular saints become signs of and for the glory of God in this world not in their individual capacity but in the context of the **communio sanctorum** in which all the participants in the eucharistic communion become "saints", thanks to their communion with the "One holy, one Lord, Jesus Christ", as the Church sings before Communion.

The problem, therefore, in every schismatic situation is not whether a certain person recognised by the one and not by the other of the separated parties as a saint really is a saint taken individually in himself. It is of no relevance in such a situation to examine whether, for example, Dioscorus or Francis of Assisi or Bernard of Clervaux, are really "saints". In a schismatic situation, such as that of the Eastern Orthodox with the Oriental Orthodox and the Roman Catholics, these persons are not actually called "saints" by the Eastern Orthodox, not because they lack "sanctity" as individuals (this, I repeat, is not the understanding of a saint by the Orthodox tradition in any case) but simply because - and this proves, I think, the point I have been trying to make here about the definition of "saint" - these "saints" do not form part of the **communio sanctorum** in which the Eastern Orthodox participate eucharistically. A "saint" is in this view a **relational** term; it ceases to exist as soon as the relationwhip is broken.

If we express this view about the "saints" in more practical terms taken from the concrete situation which exists between the Eastern and the Oriental Churches, the ecclesiological issue behind this situation becomes clear. The separation of the two Churches took place at a time when the Church, having found herself in the turmoil caused by heretical teachings, singled out from among her members doctors of the Church whom she proclaimed saints, because of the decisive guidance they offered to the Church at that critical time. But precisely because the criterion of Orthodoxy was the prevailing one, each party which was produced by divisions on issues of Orthodoxy tended to declare as saints those people anathematised by the opposite party on grounds of what was taken to be heresy. Thus the issue passed from the doctrinal to the eucharistic and ecclesiological level. Dioscorus who was anthematised by the Chalcedonian side was considered to be a saint by those who rejected Chalcedon and Leo of Rome who was anathematised by the anti-Chalcedonian party became a saint for the Chalcedonians. As a consequence of that the members of the communities of each side communicate eucharistically and ecclesiologically with saints excluded and anathematised by the other side. How can they communicate at the same Altar in such a situation?

In the Early Church this problem did not present special complications. This was due to the fact that schisms did not usually last so long as to produce the problem of "saints" in the form we are facing it now. Moreover, the usual way of healing a schism was at that time through repentence: those who repented were obliged to renounce their party entirely and this would implicitly include at least those who had been anathematised by their opponents. In later times when, for example, Oriental Orthodox joined the Roman Catholic Church in the form of Uniatism the same principle was more or less applied: Persons regarded among the Orientals as saints who happened to be anathematised by the Roman Catholic Church had to be renounced and excluded from the list of saints of the Uniate Churches.

But the way of repentance was not the only way of healing schisms in the Early Church. Some times negotiations and discussions would lead to clarifications and to final agreement between two parties, as we see, for example, in the case of the Melitian schism in the fourth century. In such a case there would be no particular dificulty in restoring full communion, as the persons involved in the division, both living or departed, who were once thought to be heretics, were no longer regarded as such. The passing from the status of heretic to that of merely schismatic, or rather the understanding that heresy did not really exist, as happened in the case of the Melitian schism, is certainly different from cases which require repentance. With this rather generalised and simplified distinction in the background, which was nevertheless firmly grounded in the tradition of the Early Church, the following categories of people involved in condemnations and needing in one way or another rehabilitation by both parties in the **communio sanctorum** before full communion might be restored could be distinguished in the history of the Early Church:

(a) Persons not officially condemned or anathematised but nevertheless not easily acceptable in the consciousness of the Church of the one party, mainly for psychological reasons. Such is the case, for example, of Theophilus of Alexandria who is revered as saint in the Oriental Churches but regarded and described in the Eastern Orthodox Synaxaria as a very bad person connected with and even responsible for persecutions against persons recognised as saints in these Synaxaria (14).

(b) Persons who are found to belong to the party condemned but who are as individuals nevertheless acceptable or even recognised as saints by the opposite party. Such is the case of deeply revered in the Oriental Churches especially among the Copts, "St. Shenouda": "who was the successor of St. Pachomius in Thebais. One could assume that the reason he was not recognised as saint in the Eastern Orthodox Church was that he happened to die after the Council of Chalcedon. A case, on the other hand, of a person recognised even as a saint by the Eastern Orthodox Churches (although he probably belonged to a party officially condemned, namely that of the Nestorians) is notably that of St. Isaac the Syrian, bishop of Ninive in the late seventh century. One may argue, of course, that we do not know enough to judge this case with certainty, but there is good reason to believe that this great spiritual father, so deeply revered in the Eastern Orthodox monastic tradition, was living in an area completely Nestorian where no possibility for his belonging to the Eastern Orthodox Church seems to have existed and was elevated to the episcopate by a Nestorian Patriarch (15).

(c) Persons revered as saints by one party but condemned by the other not for reasons of heresy. Anathematisation for reasons other than heresy was not unknown in the Early Church. Schism itself, regardless of the orthodoxy of doctrine, was considered to be equal to or perhaps more serious than heresy, and to justify the highest punishment, as we observe throughout the Novatianist and the Donatist controversies. In the case of the Oriental Churches this could apply to Dioscorus who - there is good historical reason to believe - was not condemned for heresy but for different reasons. Dioscorus is regarded as saint in the Oriental Churches.

Finally, (d) persons condemned by one of the parties for reasons of heresy but regarded by the opposite party as saints. The most typical examples of this case in the relations between Oriental and Eastern Orthodox Churches are those of Leo I or Rome, who is a saint in the Eastern Orthodox Church but condemned in the Oriental Churches, and Severus of Antioch who was condemned for heresy by the Councils recognised by the Chalcedonian Churches and revered as a great saint in the Oriental Churches.

What can be said about these categories in the light of the ecclesiological principles, common both to the Oriental and the Eastern Orthodox? It is fairly clear to me that of these categories (a) and (b) do not present unsurmountable difficulties. In the case of (a) the new psychological climate, which will have to be allowed to develop between the two parties after a common agreement on faith is announced to the people will lead to a positive re-consideration of these persons who could be regarded as local saints. Saints are in most of the cases in the Orthodox Church persons connected with a particular local community and revered especially by this community. Of course, each local community should be understood only in full unity with the rest of the communities in the world, and in this sense all saints belong to the one Catholic Church regardless of their particular association with a local community. This unity can be maintained without an expressed recognition of the saints of each community by the rest. It is enough for this unity to be maintained, if there are no serious reasons for one community to reject the saints of another. The same principles can be applied also with regard to persons under category (b) above.

The case is, of course, much more difficult with regard to categories (c) and (d). The difficulty arises from the fact that these persons have been explicitly anathematised by one of the two parties and nothing can be done unless these anathemas are lifted by the party which has imposed them or admitted also by the opposite party. The primary question, therefore, in a case like this is: If the one party is not willing to admit the anathemas imposed on it by the other party, on what grounds could these anathemas be lifted?

The broader question which lies behind this is undoubtedly that of the authority of Tradition. It is true that respect for tradition is deeply rooted in the consciousness of the Orthodox. On the other hand a careful study of the history of the Church shows that a distinction between Tradition and traditions (23) has always been maintained and applied so that the ultimate question in our case would be to what extent the anathemas with which we shall have to deal are tied up with **the** Tradition of the Church.

It is not possible in this brief paper to enter into a detailed discussion of each case. This will have to be done by a Commission at some time when the negotiations between the two parties reach the official level. Our purpose here is to point out the issues and try to underline their ecclesiological dimensions. In so doing we may make the following general observations:

In the first place a clear distinction must be made between the facts of the anathemas and the intention of the Councils which imposed them. If in the consultations so far it has been possible to distinguish the juridical and "factual" aspects of Chalcedon from the faith which it indented to proclaim and if in fact the entire progress of the discussions has been based on this distinction, could one not apply the same principle to the question of these anathemas? If persons have been anathematised on the basis of a misunderstanding of each other's doctrine could they not be restored when the real intention of the Council is recovered and agreement is reached upon it?

This principle of distinction should be studied in close connection with that of the distinction between the "Horos" and the "Canons" of a Council. Other members of this consultation have undertaken to tell us about the extent and significance of such a distinction in Orthodox Tradition. Their views can help us here clarify the question: To what extent can the Church in dealing with past anathemas treat in a special way (a) anathemas imposed for reasons other than heresy (canonical?) and (b) anathemas imposed for doctrinal views which are no longer considered to have been held by these persons?

In dealing with this question, however, we should not forget again that our very concept of Tradition is at stake. This becomes evident in a dramatic way when we consider, for example, the case of a person like Severus of Antioch. The treatment which Severus has received in Eastern Orthodox tradition goes far deeper into this tradition than his original anathematisation seems to indicate. The sixth Ecumenical Council puts him side by side with Apollinaris and calls him "impious" (a very strong expression which was linked not with behaviour but with orthodox faith). If we manage to free Severus from heretical accusations - a matter not so easy to agree upon at first sight - how can he be accepted to our common communion without clear implication on the part of the Eastern Orthodox that the sixth Ecumenical Council to which they adhere so firmly has in fact been in blunt error with regard to Severus? And if we manage to agree that

Dioscorus has been condemned not for heresy but for reasons of behaviour - a matter much easier to agree upon - how can we free him from his anathemas without implying that the same sixth Ecumenical Council by calling him "hated of God" and putting him next to Eutyches, has in fact been in error?

Such kind of difficulties coming up in dealing with anathemas and saints reveal the importance which our concept of Tradition bears in this whole matter. The real issue which is behind all this and which seems to have important ecclesiological implications is one which we might initially call **the problem of traditional minimalism**. Could we accept the possibility that what constitutes our Tradition can be reduced to a minimum and if so, what are the limitations of this? Is it enough to say that we accept only part of what constitutes the Tradition of a Church in order to have communion with this Church? Or does our refusal to accept the other part of this Tradition (e.g. the sixth Ecumenical Council) mean in fact that we refuse to enter into full communion with those who accept it? Nothing illustrates the ecclesiological importance of this question so much as the problems raised by the anathemas and the saints in our particular case here.

All this shows that the difficulties with which we are confronted on the ecclesiological level have to do to a great extent with the authority of Tradition in our Churches. This authority seems to precede the issue of canonical authority, i.e. the question of defining **who** or what organ in the Church is entitled to decide on such matters. For even if we find such an organ in, for example, what is regarded by some to be the highest authority in Orthodoxy, namely the Ecumenical Council, would our concept of Tradition allow us to expect from such a Council a repudiation or even correction of a previous Ecumenical Council? And if not, is it not perhaps of primary importance to decide first on what we mean by Tradition? Orthodoxy is by nature traditional. Yet it is an open question as to what extent this devotion to Tradition precludes adaptation of this Tradition to the particular needs and demands of historical change.

III

Another area of Church life which is affected by schism is

that known by the term **jurisdiction**. This term is loaded with juridical meaning, and when one thinks of jurisdiction it is this juridical meaning which comes immediately to mind. In fact, however, this aspect of the Church's life should not be understood apart from ecclesiology. The principles which determine jurisdiction in the Orthodox Church are to be found in ecclesiology.

The simplest overall principle in that case is that within a certain geographical area - originally the city and subsequently the diocese - the people of God should form a unity, represented by the original one eucharistic assembly under the one bishop surrounded by the presbyters. This bishop would be assisted by the deacons and "the whole Church" (Rom. 16, 23) of that area would be included. This principle was so deeply rooted in the consciousness of the primitive Church that in sources such as the writings of St. Ignatius of Antioch it is this principle which leads to the application of the term "Catholic Church" to the local community (16). This understanding of the local Church as the "Catholic Church" continues well into the fourth century as the existing sources clearly indicate (17).

The meaning of this principle is indeed most profound. The basic idea behind it is that the Church of God in her historical existence cannot ignore the realities created by the differences of culture or even nature (climatic conditions etc.) and there she cannot be conceived **in abstracto** but rather as a local Church bearing the characteristic marks of that particular geographical area. The Church on the other hand, in accepting these historical conditions, does so only in order to in fact **transcend** them in the unity that is inherent in herself, by bringing all these natural and cultural particularities up to God in the unity of the one Body of His Son, of the one people of God, just as she does in each eucharistic celebration. The uniqueness of the Eucharist as an expression of the Church's unity lies precisely in the fact that it takes on the one hand all the realities of historical existence, without ignoring or rejecting them in a pietistic manner, while on the other hand it transcends them in such a way as to prevent them from being what they are in historical existence, namely elements of division. The geographical or territorial principle, which prevailed therefore in the life of the Early Church is one of the profoundest aspects of ecclesiology.

The practical expression of this principle was to be found in the Early Church as stated in the following facts:

(a) There should be no more than one eucharistic assembly in each local community. This assembly was originally presided over by the bishop or "by whomsoever he would appoint" (18). When this became impossible to maintain later on due to practical reasons (mainly the increase of the number of Christians) and the parishes appeared as eucharistic gatherings headed by presbyters, care was taken in many highly significant ways (**Fermentum, Antimension** etc.) so that this unity of the one Eucharist in each local community of which St. Ignatius speaks be respected and maintained. Important aspects of this ecclesiological principle were also indicated by the fact that the Eucharist would never be celebrated in the Early Church by individuals (cf. the medieval and modern practice of the "private Mass" in the West) or for groups of people on the basis of their age, profession etc. (No special Eucharists for "children" or "students", for example!). The eucharistic assembly was regarded as **the catholic act par excellence of the Catholic Church in each territory**.

(b) There should not be more than one bishop in each city or diocese. This is explicitly stated by the eighth canon of I Nicaea, but its roots go deeply into the ecclesiological consciousness of the Early Church. The function of the bishop was precisely to unite in himself the various elements inherent in the local community's historical existence so that these elements might be transcended and become one in the Body of Christ, just as happens in the Eucharist of which he was the natural president. It was for this reason that not only the existence of a second bishop in the same area was regarded as a sign of schism (19) and therefore unacceptable in the Early Church, but it was also taken that each bishop was **inevitably** related to a **particular territory** by his very ordination (20) and never to a special group of people (students, armed forces, etc.) or to a special function (social service etc.) The concern behind this was deeply ecclesiological: the catholicity of the Church in each area takes into account and yet transcends the differences created by historical existence.

If this is the case in an ecclesiologically normal situation, how should the Church face the abnormalities created by schisms? What, in other words, could the Church do in trying to heal a schism which has affected this jurisdictional principle? The problem was one of the most frequent in the Early Church and we may consider some examples from that time.

The strictest way of facing the problem was never to admit at all a schismatic bishop into the ministry of the Church even if he had repented and returned. The creation and perpetuation of schism was considered to be one of the gravest offences and, as was common in all such offences repentance would allow one to communicate in the Church as a layman but not as an ordained minister. We have abundant evidence of the application of this strict discipline, for example, at the time St. Cyprian (21). This rule, however, was not without exceptions. From this same time of St. Cyprian we know for example that one of the promoters of the Novationist schism was accepted in the Church with the status of presbyter which he had had before. A condition of this, of course, was that he repented and that his acceptance was decided by a council (22).

But whether the schism was healed through repentance of the one party or through common agreement following negotiations - the latter was also known in the Early Church as we have already indicated - the principle which was maintained with a striking persistence was that after the restoration of unity there should be not more than one bishop in the same city or diocese. An example of application of this principle in case of reunion through repentance is provided by the history of Donatism. When the Council of 313 met in Rome under Miltiades to deal with Donatism outside Africa it was faced with the question of the status of those Donatist bishops which were acquitted. The decision was remarkably lenient as it provided that all Donatist bishops - except Donatus and his ten colleagues who were ordered not to return to Africa - would retain their status as bishops. When, however, this would produce two bishops in the same diocese, only he who had seniority in episcopal ordination should keep the see; for the other **alia plebs** (diocese) **regenda** should be found (23). I Nicaea in dealing with the Novationists was somewhat stricter, but when it came to the question of two bishops in the same diocese this was solved by allowing the ex-Novationist bishops to act as "chorepiscopoi" so that there would not be two bishops in the same city" (Canon 8). Another example of maintaining this principle with the same strictness, is provided by the case of the Melitian schism which had to be dealt with by I Nicaea with particular reference to the problem of the status of the Melitian clergy. The Synodical letter which is preserved by Socrates (24) provides that the Melitian bishops should keep their episcopal status but not exercise it until the see became vacant. Only after such a vacancy occurred could they be considered as the natural candidates for succession to that see.

These examples can be multiplied, but the point has become by now quite clear: Full communion for the Early Church meant also the integrity and oneness of what is now called "jurisdiction". If this practice of the Early Church had the deep ecclesiological significance which was mentioned here earlier, it is obvious that it represents something more than a mere historical situation. The ecclesiological principle behind this comes up naturally every time the question arises of a reunion of families sharing basically the same Orthodox ecclesiology.

But while this is undoubtedly an ecclesiological principle rooted deeply in Orthodox Tradition, and in that of the Early Church, our present day situation in Orthodoxy is far from being faithful to this principle. The co-existence of so many jurisdictions in the same area is, for reasons which cannot be discussed here, the prevailing practice among the Eastern Orthodox. What use is there, then, of talking about this ecclesiological principle in the dealings of the Eastern Orthodox with the Oriental Orthodox Church?

The first reasons for so doing is that the Orthodox must never cease to remind themselves of the abnormality of their situation. The more importance one attaches to this view of ecclesiology the more one feels compelled to state it vis-a-vis our realities. Another reason for mentioning this principle here is that this ecclesiological principle should not be neglected so easily in our attempts at re-establishing full communion. If full communion means what our common ecclesiology implies care must be taken so that this communion will do justice to our common vision of the Church. There may be ways to at least gradually achieve full communion without violating this vision perhaps through a mutual growing together, first on the local level. This would be the first method to be tried.

On the other hand, the from this point of view abnormal

situation in which the Orthodox Churches live today does not allow much rigidity on the matter. This abnormality may even help us to find a provisional way of dealing with the difficult ecclesiological issue which confronts us without perhaps scandalising our people. But, in view of what has been said here, any solution of this kind can be only **provisional** and accompanied by the expressed desire and intention to lead soon to an ecclesiologically normal situation.

IV

What has been said so far does not cover all the ecclesiological issues inherent in the relations between the non-Chalcedonian and the Chalcedonian Orthodox Churches. A more thorough examination of the various ecclesiological problems arising from these relations is undoubtedly necessary. It would perhaps be necessary to examine the very notion of Church unity with special reference to the problem of diversity of rite and mentality due to geographical or cultural reasons. The extent to which this diversity is permissible must be examined with special reference to the Oriental and Eastern Orthodox traditions. Another problem which was left out of consideration here is the recognition of the validity of sacramental life in each of the two sides. Both these problems could perhaps form the object of special examination, but do not in my view constitute real problems in this particular case.

What we have aimed at in this brief paper has been mainly an indication of some basic ecclesiological principles common to both the Oriental and the Eastern Orthodox Churches and an examination of some of the most difficult and thorny issues confronting us today in the light of these principles. In trying to establish these principles we have limited ourselves to what constitutes our common ecclesiological tradition going back to the time before our separation. This, I think, is a methodological principle on which we must insist, since during the long interval between our separation and the present time many important changes have taken place in our understanding of the Church.

In the light of this common ecclesiology the problems we have examined here appear to be more than mere "practical" matters to be arranged in some way or other. Neither the question of the saints nor that of jurisdiction can be isolated from our understanding of the Church. The difficulties which come up in connection with these problems cannot be overcome by some spirit of "arrangement". It is even questionable whether one could apply the practice of "Economy" to these matters. "Economy" cannot create ecclesiological realities **ex nihilo**, neither can it contradict fundamental ecclesiological principles by putting into danger the right vision of the Church.

In the same way the establishment of a certain common view of canonical authority as an instrument of judging these issues and finally overcoming them cannot be taken in itself as the right approach to the solution of these problems. Canonical authority needs proper ecclesiological justification in order to be accepted and to function in the Orthodox Church, and it cannot act and decide arbitrarily.

In connection with this, the whole problem of Tradition emerges in the discussion as perhaps the ecclesiological issue par excellence. One could say that the difficulties we are here facing on the ecclesiological level are precisely due to the fact that both sides in our dialogue take Tradition seriously, and neither side is willing to sacrifice anything from what constitutes Tradition in their eyes. Do we not need a clarification of this issue? To what extent are we prepared to re-receive our Tradition in the context of our present day situation? Without such a re-reception the ecclesiological issues we are facing will remain unsurmountable. If we intend to unite different Traditions we shall have an artificial unity. True unity of the Church requires one common Tradition as its basis.

* * *

Both Oriental and Eastern Orthodox share basically the same ecclesiology based on the vision of the Church at the time before separation. This vision was intrinsically related to a sacramental theology expressed especially in the Eucharist. It is in the light of this kind of early ecclesiology that we have tried to approach the relations of the two Churches in this paper. Other factors which have only later on in the course of history influenced the idea and structure of the Church have not been taken into consideration and should not become the decisive criteria in our efforts to restore communion.

Footnotes
1. "The Bristol Consultation" in **The Greek Orthodox Theological Review**, 13 (1968) 134.
2. Ibid. pp. 193ff.
3. Ibid. p. 134.
4. Ibid. p. 134
5. Ibid. pp. 134f.
6. Cf. the connection between martyrdom and Eucharist in St. Ignatius, **Rom.** 4, 1-2. The relationship between **martyria** and **homologia** in the consciousness of the Early Church is very instructive on this point. E.g. Matt. 10, 32; Luke 12, 8; I Tim. 6, 13 etc.
7. "The Bristol Consultation", **Ibid.**, pp. 317ff.
8. Cf. the remarkable study of W. ELERT, **Abendmahl und Kirchengemeinschaft in der alten Kirche hauptsachlich des Ostens**, 1954.
9. In the New Testament the term "saint" has precisely the meaning of membership in the community of the Church (Phil. 1, 1; Col. 1, 2; Rom. 15, 25; II Cor. 13, 12 etc.).
10. This seems to have been originally the form used in every episcopal liturgy. Today's practice of commemorating the head of the autocephalous Church to which the celebrating bishop happens to belong is an early replacement of this form which is now used only by the heads of the autocephalous Churches.
11. It is interesting that in sources like St. John Chrysostom's writings the term "synodos" is used for the Eucharistic gathering (**De Proph. obsc.** 2, 5; Migne P.G. 56, 182).
12. **Didache** 9, 4. Cf. 10, 5.
13. I Cor. 5-6.
14. See e.g. **Synaxarium Constantinopolitanum** (November), ed. by H. Delehaye, Brussels, 1902, col. 812.
15. See L. PETIT, "Isaac de Ninive" in **Dictionaire de Theologie catholique**, VIII, 10f.
16. Ignatius, **Smyr.** 8; **Eph.** 5, 1; **Philad.** 4; **Magn.** 3, 1-2.
17. For a detailed mention of these sources cf. my "The Eucharistic Community and the Catholicity of the Church" in **One in Christ**, 1970, p. 322f.
18. Ignatius, **Philad.** 4.
19. E.g. Cyrpian, **Ep.** 43 (40), 5. Cf. **De unit.** 14 and 17.
20. Even today the very prayer of ordination of a bishop

mentions explicitly the territory to which he is assigned through his ordination.
21. For example the case of Basilides and others in Cyprian, **Ep.** 55, 11; 67. Cf. Canon 2 of St. Peter of Alexandria.
22. Cyprian, **Ep.** 49.
23. Augustine, **Ep.** 43, 16.
24. H.E. I, 9.